Christ Jesus Changes Us

**Embracing True Guilt
and Breaking Free
From False Guilt**

by
Karen Watson-Jarvis, M.A., L.C.P.C.
D. Russell Bishop, Psy. D.
Mary Lou Sather, Development Editor

Copyright © 1998 by Karen Watson-Jarvis & Russell Bishop .
All rights reserved.
Electronic and soft-cover versions published by the
Wellness Institute, Inc., 1007 Whitney Ave., Gretna, LA
70056, January 1, 2000.

Cover design by the Wellness Institute, Inc.

Wellness Institute, Inc.
Gretna, LA 70056

ISBN: 1-58741-005-2
Printed in the United States Of America.

Acknowledgments

From Karen ...

With deep gratitude to Shelley
I owe the insights of this book to you.
God—Thanks for all the chances You gave and give.
What amazing grace!
Dave—My list and more. Let's grow in grace together.

From Russell ...

Thanks to all the clients who have
helped give me insight into the healing process.

Thanks to my family for putting up with my dreams
and helping them to come true.

Table of Contents

Introduction vi

Chapter One
    God's Radical Blueprint for Change 1

Chapter Two
    God Knows What We Need 7

Chapter Three
    Avoiding True Guilt: Running from Grace 23

Chapter Four
    Indulging in False Guilt: Running from Grace 43

Chapter Five
    The Healing Process 61

Chapter Six
    Healing for the Avoider 73

Chapter Seven
    Healing for the Indulger 91

Chapter Eight
    Talking to Family Members 115

Chapter Nine
    Perspectives for Professionals who Offer Healing 125

Chapter Ten
    The Church and the Healing Process 147

Chapter Eleven
    Final Words to Encourage 155

Introduction

Karen's Story

"She looks so put together." "Karen never really seems to have any problems." "You have so much energy." "You are so kind and giving." For much of my life similar statements shaped a large portion of my self-image. These ideas kept me stuck, hungering for the wrong ways to feel good about myself. Then my world began to crumble. The effectiveness of being "all put together" became ineffective one day.

I was always a chronically busy person, working nearly full-time. I was a full-time student, had a boyfriend, rode my bike several miles a day. I also filled my time with early morning prayer meetings, Wednesday and Sunday church services, and Bible study groups.

I lived with the belief that I was a warm and supportive friend, until my closest friend started pointing out my critical nature. She would share her deep pain with me, crying and telling me how much I was hurting her. Instead of hearing her, I would fill my mind with destructive rebuttals: "Where do you come off telling me I'm hurting you? Who are you to say such things to me? Do you think you're so perfect and the world's greatest friend? The problem with *you* is that you're too sensitive. You are really the one with problems, not me. Can you find another person in this entire world who would agree that I'm a bad friend? I'll tell you the answer to that. The answer is, 'No!'" Such thinking was destroying our friendship.

I refused to hear her because subconsciously I believed that recognizing my critical conduct would destroy our relationship. I blocked out what my friend said and continued to hurt her. Finally, after numerous unsuccessful attempts to reach me, my friend stated she would end our friendship if I did not change. I was enraged. I thought, "How dare she threaten me? If anyone has a right to leave this relationship it is me." But I truly did not want to lose my best friend.

One day I went to an amusement park with a guy who treated me for eight hours as critically as I had treated my best friend for over two years. At the end of the day, I thought indignantly, "No one deserves to be treated this way." At that point, God broke my heart and revealed my folly, leaving me with deep sorrow for the wounds I now knew I had caused my best friend. I went home and shared with her what God had shown me, and the specific ways I realized I had wronged her. The paradox was that I did not lose our friendship. All she had ever wanted was for me to care about her and to stop hurting her. She could immediately see the change that the God of grace had brought in my heart. I am forever grateful both to my friend and to God for taking me on this journey of healing.

Russell's Story

I have always been concerned with details and making sure that I am doing all that I can to be responsible. I have often labored to do more, to assure myself that others would accept me, and most importantly, that God would accept me. I was afraid God was continually displeased with the way I fell short of what I assumed to be His expectations. I was unable to take comfort in His grace and His provisions.

Worry has long been a trait of mine. I believed that thinking through all possible solutions to a problem would ensure my success. I would spend hours planning and rehearsing for eventualities that usually never came. I can remember feeling that God would be more pleased if only I memorized more scriptures, had longer devotions, or became more involved in church activities. If I missed a devotional time, I felt distant from God and as though I had really let Him down. I could not allow myself to accept God's promises to provide for my needs. I felt that I had to be the constant giver to others and that my own needs were selfish. I believed God needed me to be perfect before I would be good enough to receive the fulfillment of His promises.

My worries often left me worn and frightened, for my best efforts to control events and outcomes were often not enough. I felt disappointed and was sure I had failed to live up to God's standards. Rather than focusing on God's grace, His perfect acceptance of me and provisions for my needs, I became apathetic and despairing. I was stuck over and over again in the mire of shame and false guilt. I would long for God's comfort, but I usually thought only that He expected more from me. I was on a crash course for burnout and anxiety attacks.

When I finally realized God's grace and comfort, my anxiety and tension began to disappear. I learned to rely on God's promises of acceptance, and that He would provide for my needs. Although I have not yet "arrived" in my own healing process, I continue to experience God's love in exciting new ways.

Interestingly, these two stories illustrate some of the difficulties encountered in life by the two prevailing personality types we will be addressing in this book. That the stories are our own as authors is an indication of the widespread occurrence of these personality quirks, and are examples of the all-encompassing need each one of us has for God's healing, restoring grace. We invite you to join us in this journey toward hearing God's individual message, tailored in His love and grace to fit you and me specifically.

Chapter One
God's Radical Blueprint for Change

Have you ever felt enmeshed in a web of personal turmoil? Does everyone you know seem to be handling life better than you are? Perhaps you are constantly being badly treated by family and friends. Perhaps you continually struggle with being unable to live up to others' expectations. Maybe your life is burdened by guilt or disillusionment. God wants to meet you at the point of your need and provide the special healing He has crafted to fit you alone. Come with us on this journey into healing your emotions God's way.

Many of us become trapped by guilt, whether we are avoiding or indulging in it. Until we recognize the positive aspects of guilt and identify its negative components, we can't move forward in the healing process. We must also be willing to move out of our personal comfort zones and learn new ways of interacting with everyone around us. As we risk the discomfort of change, God enters our struggles with us and brings hope and freedom to our lives that had seemed doomed and mired in confusion.

As we examine God's radical blueprint for change, we will identify two different responses to guilt. People who seek at all costs to deflect their guilt onto others and who constantly deny responsibility for their own actions can be called Avoiders of true guilt. Others, who experience guilt as a motivator toward repentance, experience true guilt. Some of these, however, may focus on personal guilt to the point that their relationships with God and those around them are obstructed, and they may take responsibility for things that are outside their control or obligation. These persons may be referred to as Indulgers in false guilt. Throughout this book we will consider together the way God speaks to each person's response to guilt, whether avoiding or indulging.

Profiles of Avoiders of True Guilt

Repeatedly, John told Kim that her critical comments hurt him deeply. As she listened, she thought, "John is too sensitive. He deserves to be insulted because he hurts me, too. John always makes such a big deal out of nothing. I deserve someone who appreciates me. I can't help what I do. It's John's problem, not mine." Her behavior toward him remained unchanged.

Kim was an Avoider of true guilt. She rationalized and justified her poor treatment of John even when he tried to share his pain with her. As she shifted the focus away from her own actions, she avoided her real guilt, which could have moved her toward repentance and reconciliation in her relationship with John.

Avoiders of true guilt downplay or refuse to accept responsibility for the ways their actions hurt others. They choose in overt or subtle ways to ignore the true realities of their sin. Personal responsibility is then forfeited. Avoiders of true guilt focus on the actions of others to avoid their need to love others the way God loves them.

Tools of the Avoider

Some examples of Avoider's tactics include: blaming others when you are the one with the problem, rationalizing hurtful conduct, justifying behavior patterns, or making excuses to mask the ugliness of your sin. Other schemes may be choosing to hide problems, embracing secrecy to avoid being discovered, maintaining a critical spirit to prevent self-examination, and being unwilling to see the damage caused by your actions toward another.

Avoider Number Two

Ron believed he was entitled to happiness, and deserved to be treated "right." He felt stuck in his 6-year marriage and had lost his love for his wife. He lied to her about his affairs, as he believed that these other women were God's gift to him for putting up with his wife for all those years. He told himself that no one ever needed to know about his affairs and thus no one would be hurt, and he developed elaborate scenarios in his head to justify what he was doing. He told himself that he felt good for the first time in a long time and that was all he cared about. When his wife discovered his unfaithfulness, he told her it was her fault. If she had only met his needs, he would have had no need for the affairs. He also blamed his parents' treatment of him for causing his pain, and refused to hear of the pain he was bringing to his wife and their families.

Avoider Number Three

Tom was 16 years old, and was tired of his parents telling him what to do. As he mentally recounted their unfair treatment, he was determined to get back at them and show them how badly they had behaved toward him. He vowed he would teach them to stop trying to control him. He got an outlandish haircut to spite his parents. He stole money from them, refused any church activities and said cruel things about his family to anyone who would listen.

These examples give some of the characteristics of Avoiders of true guilt.

Profiles of Indulgers in False Guilt

Josh was often beaten by his father. Josh believed that he caused his father's rage when he disagreed or became angry with his father. When he tried to tell his father how he was affected by these rages, his father would tell Josh that he was an ungrateful child who was cruel and unkind He would tell Josh he did not want to hit him, but that Josh deserved it. Josh believed he was undeserving of love and isolated himself, drawing away from others and believing he would make their lives miserable and difficult if his life impacted theirs. Josh constantly felt worthless. He would apologize for any real or imagined mistakes he made, and believed he deserved awful punishment for his many errors.

Indulgers in false guilt feel overly responsible for things they cannot realistically control. Those who suffer false guilt fail to see themselves as precious and deserving of God's love. They focus on others because they feel little sense of personal worth. Many coping tools are used by those who fail to love themselves the way God loves them. Some examples of these mechanisms are: blaming themselves for another's problems, having few personal boundaries, and allowing others to take advantage of them. They also often critically attack themselves, and work too hard to make others like them. In addition they avoid caring for themselves for fear of being selfish.

Indulger Number Two

Carrie grew up with an alcoholic father. Her husband treated her with respect in the early years of their marriage but later became a workaholic and avoided their home. Carrie tried desperately to attract her husband to come home to her. She would create elaborate dinners, dress in ways he liked, be on her best behavior. She sacrificed her own needs in a vain attempt to make him happy. Despite her best efforts her husband was never satisfied, leaving Carrie overwhelmed with loneliness. He told her he would leave if he ever found out that she spoke badly of him to anyone, so she kept all her pain inside herself, weeping all alone. She gave to everyone else, but found she couldn't accept compliments or gifts from anyone because she didn't believe she was worthy of them. When friends asked how she was doing she would say, "fine" and would try endlessly to be available if they needed her.

Indulger Number Three

In desperation Tina went to a pastor to share the pain inflicted by her husband's numerous affairs. She confided that he avoided sex with her and she felt ashamed and unworthy as a wife. The pastor blamed her for the affairs. He told her that what her husband was doing was not wrong and that she needed to learn to love and accept her husband for who he was. She also needed to stop being so controlling and manipulative. He told her that she was too angry to think clearly and needed to forgive her husband and ask him to forgive her for wanting him to change. She accepted what the pastor said and felt that it was her Christian duty to support her husband even though she felt sickened by his infidelity. She decided never again to share her pain and anger with anyone else, believing that others would see her as the pastor did. She began having anxiety attacks and believed they were God's punishment for her not being a better wife and Christian.

These Indulgers in false guilt were unable to experience God's compassionate love. As they took responsibility for the actions of others, they masked or evaded their own neediness.

Christ's Touch Changes Us

Chapter Two
God Knows What We Need

As God speaks to people in scripture, He uses two radically different styles: gentle and bold. These two approaches are tailored to the divergent responses of different people. Each method provides an opportunity for the individual to experience His specific grace. People avoid or curtail their change process when they prefer to remain comfortable, hearing only what they want to hear from God instead of receiving His call to restoration. Insensitivity to God's messages inhibits His healing and grace.

God and the Indulger

God is tender, patient and gentle with persons who live overwhelmed with guilt that is not theirs to carry. Jesus spoke to the woman at the well and to the woman caught in adultery with tenderness and compassion. Each needed to hear His message enveloped in gentle mercy. Jesus also demonstrated patience and forbearance when He dealt with His disciple Peter.

God and the Avoider

Conversely, God confronts those who ignore or avoid true guilt in their lives. He often uses harsh measures to get the attention of those who ignore his leading. The Old Testament describes how God repeatedly led His people into exile in order to redirect them toward Him. Jesus spoke boldly and forcefully to the self-satisfied Pharisees throughout His ministry. Through the writing and ministry of the apostle Paul, God spoke pointedly to the members of the Corinthian church as He guided their growth.

God's character is consistent and does not change, despite how we may feel from day to day. Exploring several aspects of God's character will reveal how He speaks differently to meet the specific needs of different types of people. Scripture describes this wisdom of God in 1 Corinthians 2:6-10:

We do, however, speak a message of wisdom among the mature, but not the wisdom of this age or of the rulers of this age, who are coming to nothing. No, we speak of God's secret wisdom, a wisdom that has been hidden and that God destined for our glory before time began. None of the rulers of this age understood it, for if they had, they would not have crucified the Lord of Glory. However, as it is written: "No eye has seen, no ear has heard, no mind has conceived what God has prepared for those who love him:"—but God has revealed to us by his spirit. The spirit searches all things, even the deep things of God.

God's character is far beyond our understanding, but is one that always operates out of passion and love for our well being.

Other passages describe the character of God as One Who requires our participation to determine His responses. Mark 9:43 states the need to choose salvation. Matthew 10:32-33 points out the need to chose to listen to God in order to have peace, and Isaiah 48:16-18 describes the choice to be stubborn, disbelieve, and speak evil.

People often distort the message God intends. Those who need tenderness hear harshness, while those who need confrontation hear a gentle message that does not break through their psychological defenses. Typically, growth and change are uncomfortable and often painful. God wants our change rather than our comfort. We unfortunately prefer comfort to change and thereby thwart God's plan for our healing.

Comfort zones are unhealthy habitual patterns that keep us from experiencing God's best for us by perpetuating habits of mediocrity and sameness. Staying in one's comfort zones promotes a false sense of safety and security that doesn't allow for emotional or spiritual growth. Sensitivity to God's particular message for you will lead you to be able to embrace His grace and move ahead in your healing process.

Scripture outlines the need to choose: From Eve's choice in Genesis to eat the forbidden fruit, to the choice described in the last chapter of Revelation: "Whoever is thirsty, let him come; and whoever wishes, let him take the free gift of the water of life." (22:17) Every step in life is full of choices, from humbling ourselves so we can receive God's love (2 Chronicles 7:14) to choosing to be close and intimate with Him (Psalm 145:18). Each of our choices in these areas has lifelong effects.

Another Avoider

Mark came into the office fed up with God. He had stopped going to church and pushed his Bible study friends away. He knew that God called him to obey the government but decided God asked too much from him. He then avoided paying his taxes for three years and was caught by the IRS. He began to realize that God would not force him to follow Him and that choosing his own path led to destructive behaviors. Mark came to see this reality only with difficulty because when he did, he was forced to confront his own responsibility for his life.

God gives some answers describing what He will do in response to our choices. Not all of His answers to our choices are pleasant. Discipline and even harshness clearly result when we make choices that push us away from Him and His divine will. Again, it is important to realize that He wants our choices to allow us to embrace His love.

God always chooses to discipline us for our good, and lovingly treats us as His children (Hebrews 12:4-13). We often carry distorted ideas about what God's discipline is composed of. A loving mother in her greater wisdom knows that antiseptic on a wound may sting, but it also helps to heal. Her child will not understand the love she displays when she applies the uncomfortable medication. At that moment the child will see his mother as uncaring and cruel, because the child does not have the perspective of the loving parent.

God tenderly realizes that we often don't understand His way or the love behind His actions. His character moves Him to put spiritual antiseptic on our open wounds, because to ignore them would be unloving and contrary to His nature. Whether or not the child ever understands what the parent had done, her character, as God's character, is still the same.

God never enables us to stay sick or stuck in destructive behaviors. In His desire not to harm us by enabling unhealthy patterns, He instead withdraws His active support from our daily lives until we take responsible steps toward healing. God does not promise a quick fix, but He offers concrete help and power for those who are willing to follow His way and seek His help. When we are sincere, He is immediately there in power and abundance.

> Come near to God and he will come near to you. Wash your hands, you sinners, and purify your hearts, you double-minded. (James 4:8)

God will always forgive when we show clear willingness to acknowledge our sin, a desire to be purified and free from it, and a longing to restore relationships broken by sin. In addition to forgiving us, He will draw near in intimacy. He also promises never to hold repented sins against us.

Grace: A Choice

God will always offer hope and grace to those who want it, but it is essential to want it. When we have a deep desire for something in life, we are usually willing to do whatever it takes to attain it. When we aren't willing to pay the price, rewards do not follow. The deepest reality of choice is that the same God who loved us enough to send Jesus Christ to die on the cross, must watch in agony as those He loves descend into the "Pit of Hell" or eternal separation from Him, because they have not chosen His way. He never forces choice. He does not send only the sins themselves to Hell, He rather sends the sinful person there because of his or her hardened heart. He, in the end, does not separate the sin from the sinner. His grace still sends people to Hell, and grasping that difficult concept can radically change lives. Harshness is God's way of responding to Avoiders of true guilt. His way awakens the need to destroy self-centeredness, and to love others.

Matthew 5:43-46 states,
> You have heard that it was said, 'Love your neighbor and hate your enemy,' But I tell you: love your enemies and pray for those who persecute you, that you may be sons of your Father in heaven. He causes his sun to rise on the evil and the good, and sends rain on the righteous and the unrighteous. If you love those who love you, what reward will you get? Are not even the tax collectors doing that?

And Philippians 2:2-4:
> Then make my joy complete by being like-minded, having the same love, being one in spirit and purpose. Do nothing out of selfish ambition or vain conceit, but in humility consider others better than yourselves. Each of you should look not only to your own interests, but also to the interests of others.

The key issue in both of these passages is the need for us to change our self-centered thinking. God knows Avoiders of true guilt will never choose to love others unless it somehow results in some personal gain, and He confronts this pattern. God states that until we are willing to love the unlovely and those who hate us, our love is not real. Remember, God is speaking to a particular audience. These passages would be counter-productive for those who indulge in false guilt.

God's grace is essential to His character, but in His wisdom He knows that some people will experience the reality of grace through harshness. 1 Peter 2:16 tells us we need to "live as free men, but do not use your freedom as a cover up for evil; live as servants of God." Jude 1:4 states,

They are godless men, who change the grace of our God into a license for immorality and deny Jesus Christ our only Sovereign and Lord.

Our task as humans is to accept God's character in all its complexities. We must accept His grace. We are all different however, and God uses different tactics to approach us and get our attention. God uses harsh tactics to approach Avoiders of true guilt. The Avoider of true guilt has a propensity to use both people and God:

> Or do you show contempt for the riches of his kindness, tolerance and patience, not realizing that God's kindness leads you toward repentance? But because of your stubbornness and your unrepentant heart, you are storing up wrath against yourself for the day of God's wrath, when his righteous Judgment will be revealed. (Romans 2:4-5)

God's reality is that wrath is deserved. Our desire for kindness, forbearance and patience allows avoidance of the real issue, but God knows that the needed issue is repentance.

Results of Avoidance

Failing to love others and avoiding true guilt produce their own consequences. Romans 11:22-24 also addresses the coexisting kindness and sternness of God. God chooses to be stern to those who are choosing a path away from Him. John 5:14 states, "See, you are well again. Stop sinning or something worse may happen to you." Here God is warning those who would avoid looking at their sin. His warnings are designed to avert the progression of sin and its damaging effects.

God challenges the Avoider of true guilt to look honestly at issues of deception. Justifying and rationalizing sin is wrong in God's eyes, and He has much to say about it:

> Everyone who sins breaks the law; in fact, sin is lawlessness. But you know that he appeared so that he might take

away our sins. And in him is no sin. No one who continues to sin has either seen him or known him. (1 John 3:4-6)

So I say, live by the spirit, and you will not gratify the desires of the sinful nature. For the sinful nature desires what is contrary to the spirit, and the Spirit what is contrary to the sinful nature. (Galatians 5:16-17)

The propensity to deny, rationalize, and blame issues away is a serious matter. God's response is that when sins continue, His grace and His will are shunted aside.

God also talks harshly about living a double life. Avoiders of true guilt often have dramatically different double lives. One personality presentation may appear to be loving and dynamic. In the next moment, the individual can be cruel, manipulative and abusive. God confronts our choosing to see only good in ourselves when too many other areas of our lives show a serious lack of compassion or love for others.

Doublemindedness is incredibly deceptive. We often have pastors or Christian leaders come through our clinic who have dramatically and dishonestly chosen to separate the sins in their life from their Christian ministry. Doublemindedness blinds the sinner to the reality that the same apparently loving and caring person is committing the sin:

Therefore, get rid of all moral filth and the evil that is so prevalent and humbly accept the word planted in you, which can save you. Do not merely listen to the word, and so deceive yourselves. Do what it says. Anyone who listens to the word but does not do what it says is like a man who looks at his face in a mirror and, after looking at himself, goes away and immediately forgets what he looks like. But the man who looks intently into the perfect law that gives freedom, and continues to do this, not forgetting what he has heard, but doing it—he will be blessed in what he does. (James 1:21-25)

The case of Kim in Chapter One illustrates this point. She initially would listen to her husband John and begin to get a picture of what she looked like, but then she would immediately resort to rationalizing, blaming, and self-preoccupation, thus losing her ability to see her own reality.

> If we claim to have fellowship with him yet walk in the darkness, we lie and do not live by the truth. But if we walk in the light as he is in the light, we have fellowship with one another, and the blood of Jesus, his Son, purifies us from all sin. If we claim to be without sin, we deceive ourselves and the truth is not in us. If we confess our sins, he is faithful and just and will forgive us our sins and purify us from all unrighteousness. If we claim we have not sinned, we make him out to be a liar and his word has no place in our lives. (1 John 1:6-10)

Avoider Self-Deception

The guilt-Avoider finds it easy to deceive him or herself. In one breath sin appears to be acknowledged, but in the next breath comes total denial. The case of Ron illustrates this point. He avoided the wrong of what he was doing by saying that it was his wife's fault, and that he deserved happiness. God challenges us to embrace the sin and ugliness of our actions fully, and then He is free to forgive and purify. Unfortunately, few Avoiders choose confession, self-examination, repentance, and restitution, preferring a pattern of deception. God is angry when evil is avoided, and outward life that looks good will never fool Him. Avoiders choose to buy the lie that sin is justified, unfortunately at the cost of avoiding God's grace. God's warning is that good done in deception will never cover evil. The sad reality is that in deception, grace and forgiveness are forfeited, always at a cost to ourselves and to others.

Love: A Definition

God challenges the Avoider of true guilt to examine what love is. He defines love in ways foreign to those who fail to love others.

> This is how we know what love is: Jesus Christ laid down his life for us. And we ought to lay down our lives for our brothers. If anyone has material possessions and sees his brother in need but has no pity on him, how can the love of God be in him? Dear children, let us not love with words and speech, but in action and in truth. (1 John 3:16-18)

God defines love for the Avoider of true guilt by looking at the need to restore love for others. He challenges the Avoider's need to be self-absorbed. Avoiders can be present in a worship service designed to convict them to give to others, and they will quickly be able to ignore the conviction. God knows a heart of compassion is essential; such a heart needs to be cultivated in order to continue the journey toward loving others. Avoiders of true guilt do give to others at times, not as a means to care about them, but as a way to call attention to their own generosity. Avoiders choose to deceive, to use others and to show the face they want others to see. This deceptive caring simply reinforces their double-mindedness. God sees each heart and knows convicting love is needed, and will allow painful consequences for an unwillingness to hear.

> [Avoiders] claim to know God, but by their actions they deny him. They are detestable, disobedient and unfit for anything good. (Titus 1:16)

These are strong words of condemnation. God will never allow hypocrisy to replace true love. He does not accept double-mindedness, but sees the whole package as evil.

God appears to speak harshly to inspire growth and discipline, and to draw the Avoider away from self-centeredness. He speaks harshly to those who are stubborn and unrepentant of the sins they commit against God and others. Those who avoid true guilt rationalize, justify and minimize sin to avoid seeing hurt to God, and anyone else. Blaming others becomes a way of life.

God chooses discipline and harshness as an effective way to break through denial and self-centeredness. He wants all of us to embrace a better life, a life enriched by peace, righteousness, and grace.

Grace for the Indulger

God uses gentle tactics to draw those who indulge in false guilt into a closer relationship with Him. Unlike Avoiders, Indulgers in false guilt often view God as overly harsh and demanding. They believe God is to be feared and that by working harder or doing more, they can gain His favor. God recognizes that these individuals would be crushed or driven away by harshness, so He speaks tenderly and softly to their needs.

God's tender, compassionate message is the healing balm for Indulgers in false guilt. Jesus reached out in tenderness throughout His healing ministry. Jesus spoke to the woman at the well on His way through Samaria. This woman was deeply troubled and had apparently attempted to soothe her own pain through sexual relationships. Rather than bluntly confronting her behavior, Jesus reached out to her neediness and offered a solution to her unquenched thirst for intimacy. He offered permanent healing. She responded to His tender message by telling others what Jesus had done for her.

Further Grace

In another situation, Jesus demonstrated compassion in the face of social pressure. He was eating at the house of a Pharisee when a woman approached him and began to wash His feet. It was customary to wash the dust and grime from one's feet after traveling but Jesus' host had not provided Him this service. This woman broke with custom not only by washing His feet herself, but by using expensive perfume for the washing and by drying Jesus' feet with her own hair. She was ridiculed by the host, who also challenged Jesus' judgment in the situation. Jesus' response was to rebuke the self-righteous host while tenderly supporting the woman's actions. He thus enabled the woman to experience God's grace through His compassion, as she had demonstrated sacrificial servanthood to Him by her behavior.

The most striking example of tenderness leading to grace may be seen through the account of the woman caught in adultery. Jesus confronted the Pharisees who were about to stone this woman, for she had clearly broken the law and under the law deserved this punishment. He challenged them to examine their own lives and to go ahead and stone her if they themselves were blameless before God. The woman was not stoned. Jesus instructed her to go and not commit adultery again. Through tenderness He directed her to grace, not by accusation as the Pharisees had done.

More Tenderness

Peter's experience with Christ is another example of tenderness that radically changed a defeated man who felt like a failure after denying his Lord. Peter vowed to Jesus that he would rather die than betray Him. In a moment of fear for his life, Peter did what he had sworn he would not do. He betrayed Jesus not once, but three times. He walked away feeling worthless and useless for God's kingdom. Jesus returned and tenderly dismissed Peter's inadequacy by emphasizing his value to the kingdom of God. He confronted Peter's failure with kindness and understanding toward a heart broken by sin and betrayal. God gave Peter a priceless gift at a time Peter felt totally undeserving.

Guilt as a Positive

One of God's essential means of showing us His way is through quilt. Most of us consider quilt as negative, but God uses feelings of true guilt as a tool to keep us from repeating actions that hurt Him, others, and ourselves. Guilt is a necessary component of morality and helps us to balance right and wrong actions, motivating us toward godliness. Through conscience God develops in us sensitivity to His leading. Biblical principles stand in direct contrast to the present society where truth is considered relative. Thus guilt is a positive feeling used by God to redirect us.

Guilt is a combination of: regret, sadness, or remorse and thoughts such as: It was my fault. I should not have done that! These feelings and thoughts motivate us to avoid repeating the same destructive action. The level of our experienced guilt may result from the seriousness of the wrong, the workings of our conscience, or our emotional makeup. True guilt is God's tool to prevent us from repeatedly doing things that hurt Him, others, and ourselves. Guilt is the signal to alert us that we are stepping outside of God's grace and protection.

God intends guilt to have the same effect for everyone because it reflects His unchanging standards. He does approach us in divergent ways and we respond differently to His messages. Guilt is not meant to take away fun, hinder pleasure, or to be oppressive. God is ultimately invested in using guilt as a corrective to guide us closer to Him.

Guilt helps us to make moral decisions. Intellectually accepting moral standards is the first element in moral decision-making. Knowing, for example, that murder is against the sixth commandment (Exodus 20:13) is important to formulating decisions not to murder.

A definition of murder sometimes is not clear or straightforward, such as during war or an action of self-defense. Guilt feelings help us to find a balance in the moral decision-making process. This balancing act is also aided by the development of conscience, a concept which will be detailed later.

Guilt serves to motivate us to proper action. In the legal sense, a person found guilty of a violation is sentenced to take responsible action to pay for the violation. Guilt feelings may also convict a person to take responsibility for a violation, and to repent and make restitution. Feeling guilty about having committed a violation can help the person avoid repeating the action. Some people, however, will not feel guilty even though they indeed did do the action, while others may feel excessively guilty even though they actually did nothing wrong. These alternate responses to guilt exemplify Avoiders of true guilt and Indulgers in false guilt.

Christian Life-Balance

Balanced sensitivity to guilt is crucial to the successful Christian life:

> Timothy, my son, I give you this instruction in keeping with the prophecies once made about you, so that by following them you may fight the good fight, holding on to faith and a good conscience. Some have rejected these and so have shipwrecked their faith. (1 Timothy 1:18-19)

The viability of our faith is at risk when we neglect building our sensitivity to guilt.

Consider that sinking feeling in the pit of your stomach or that lump in your throat when you hear sirens and see the flashing lights of the squad car in your rearview mirror. Few of us are happy to give the officer our driver's license and vehicle registration. For most of us these are tense moments.

People will have different responses to these types of situations. Some become incensed and angry, attempting to blame the officer or someone else, focusing on issues other than going 48 miles per hour in a 35 mile per hour speed zone. This person may rant and rave or attempt to intimidate by telling the officer names of persons he or she knows at city hall who can "fix" the ticket. These reactions represent the Avoider of true guilt. Avoiders do not wish to face the consequences of their actions. Guilt in this situation is not used in a beneficial way—to motivate turning away from the unsafe behavior, which in this case is speeding.

The Indulger and Guilt

Another response to the traffic stop scenario illustrates the Indulger in false guilt. Reactions for the Indulger may include tearful sobs, multiple apologies, and repeated negative self thoughts such as: "I am a terrible driver." "I never pay attention when I am supposed to." "I don't deserve to drive on my own." These reactions are self-effacing and overburdensome. The Indulger's response likely leaves him or her mentally paralyzed, emotionally unable to meet other responsibilities later that day because the guilt experience is overwhelming. The Indulger may attempt to undo the violation by driving 10 miles per hour under the speed limit for the next week.

The positive aspect of guilt in this speed limit example illustrates the motivation to pay more attention to the speed limit and drive accordingly. Following our conscience breeds self respect. The apostle Paul spoke of feeling positively about himself because he had lived consistently with his values (Acts 23:1).

Forgiveness Across the Spectrum of Guilt

Guilt is a tool used by God to point us in a new direction. It can provide motivation to change, but in itself has no power actually to change the state of affairs. Forgiveness is God's direct application of His grace to violations. In Psalm 103 we find compassionate forgiveness to be part of God's character. He is interested in providing us a means of correcting our shortcomings. We simply need to accept His offer:

> If we confess our sins, he is faithful and just and will forgive us our sins and purify us from all unrighteousness. (1 John 1:9)

Forgiveness is distorted by both the Avoider and Indulger. The Avoider fails to acknowledge the need for forgiveness and is invested in overlooking or ignoring guilt's reminder call to repentance. The Indulger mistakenly tries to use guilt as the method for correction, viewing the power to correct in direct proportion to the amount of guilt experienced: a little guilt yields a little correction, while massive guilt yields massive correction. Both perspectives discount God's role in offering His forgiveness as the corrective solution.

When True Guilt is Distorted

Some people experience more guilt than others when they do something wrong in large part because of their development of conscience. Conscience is a gift God gives to all people and is both spiritual and psychological in nature. Our conscience is the place God pricks with guilt feelings and thoughts that motivate us to different action.

Some individuals have a markedly limited capacity for conscience. Serial killers such as Jeffrey Dahmer, Richard Speck, or Son of Sam represent extreme examples of this type of individual. These persons are not able fully to appreciate the devastation resulting from their behavior. They have a severely stunted ability to experience remorse for their destructive actions toward others.

God's message is conveyed to us in the way we are most likely to be able to hear it. We also develop responses to God's directives which lead us to distort His message. When we deny or distort our own guilt, we impede God's grace and healing in our lives. We also may come to distort our view of God in the process, viewing Him as a vengeful God just waiting to pour out His wrath on us when we fail His expectations, or conversely, viewing Him as an all benevolent God with no corrective intentions for our lives. Either perspective is extreme and blocks our balanced relationship with God.

God knows our innermost needs. Through the character of Christ He has shown us that He will reach out to us and speak to us in ways sensitive to our imperfections Unfortunately, we often distort God's message, hearing only what we want to hear, in the way we want to hear it. God uses quilt to motivate us to positive choices and offers forgiveness as a correction of our shortcomings.

Despite God's intention for guilt to bring positive results, people instead become trapped by it, either avoiding it or indulging in it. It is very important that we as Christians seek to build our sensitivity to true guilt. True guilt always points toward repentance and to a restored relationship with God Who longs to shower us with His grace. Chapters three and four discuss how we distort God's message and stay trapped in our comfort zones. People become encased in guilt, either avoiding it or indulging in it. As you approach these chapters it will be important to examine yourself carefully, striving to be aware of how you or someone you know may be missing God's best in life.

Chapter Three
Avoiding True Guilt: Running from Grace

The Avoider of true guilt ignores the call of God to repentance. He or she uses many tactics to shift the focus of attention away from his or her behavior to the behavior of others, and to external circumstances. Indulgers in false guilt thus often fall prey to the Avoider's blame and defocusing. This chapter explores the characteristics of the Avoider, showing how he or she diminishes God's grace by avoiding His call to repentance.

Self Quiz

The following list details the main traits seen in the Avoider of true guilt. Check those items which describe your own behavior. A positive response to several of these items raises the question that you may have issues related to avoiding true guilt.

Avoider Self Quiz

1) Occasionally use scripture to avoid my own responsibility. "If you don't forgive me, God won't forgive you!"   YES____ NO____

2) Shift blame to others. "I know I did, but you did....   YES____ NO____

3) Feel reactive and destructive when I am told I hurt others.   YES____ NO____

4) Ignore God's desire for purity in thoughts and actions.   YES____ NO____

5) Take pride in not being able to be put down by others. YES____ NO____

6) Feel entitled to good things, feeling unfairly treated by life. YES____ NO____

7) Be unwilling to pardon or forgive others when they hurt me. Hold a grudge. YES____ NO____

8) Demand unconditional love even though I don't love back. YES____ NO____

9) Feel clever when I can "bend the rules." YES____ NO____

10) Feel angry when others challenge me to change. Accuse them of judging. YES____ NO____

11) Put down people who irritate me. YES____ NO____

12) Convince others to feel sorry for how I am mistreated. YES____ NO____

13) Be demanding and critical of others. YES____ NO____

14) Make excuses when I have been caught doing something wrong. YES____ NO____

15) Feel that people expect too much from me. YES____ NO____

16) Need to feel in control in every situation. Want things "my way." YES____ NO____

17) Become angry when I have to face consequences for my actions. YES____ NO____

18) Don't believe I need help. Get irritated when
help is suggested.   YES____ NO____

19) Become angry when people do not believe
I've changed, and do not trust me.   YES____ NO____

20) Lie to minimize or avoid consequences for my
actions.   YES____ NO____

A caveat with this self-assessment should be noted. Avoiders of true guilt are invested in ignoring the negatives in their own behavior, and especially the way this negative behavior hurts others. Those truly interested in learning about themselves may wish to take the self assessment a step further, asking several close friends and family to rate the behaviors on this list. These individuals will be able to provide a more frank assessment of the Avoiders' characteristics. If friends give a different response than your spouse does this should be a danger signal. If the notion of approaching others seems too discomforting to pursue, this discomfort many in itself be a clue indicating that you have issues related to avoiding true guilt.

Abusing Forgiveness

God is deeply concerned about forgiveness. The entire focus of human history is oriented around God's redemptive actions through Jesus Christ. God's purposes for forgiveness are often abused by the Avoider who uses forgiveness to his or her advantage. The Avoider views forgiveness as something which she or he deserves to receive, yet giving forgiveness is not important. In contrast, Indulgers in false guilt often focus on indebtedness and strive to forgive even when it is not necessary or appropriate.

An example of how the Avoider misrepresents and misappropriates forgiveness is seen in the parable of the unmerciful servant found in Matthew 18:23-35,

Therefore, the kingdom of heaven is like a king who wanted to settle accounts with his servants. As he began the settlement, a man who owed him ten thousand talents was brought to him. Since he was not able to pay, the master ordered that he and his wife and his children and all that he had be sold to repay the debt. The servant fell on his knees before him. 'Be patient with me,' he begged, 'and I will pay back everything.' The servant's master took pity on him, canceled the debt and let him go. But when that servant went out, he found one of his fellow servants who owed him a hundred denarii. He grabbed him and began to choke him. 'Pay back what you owe me!' he demanded. His fellow servant fell to his knees and begged him, 'Be patient with me, and I will pay you back. 'But he refused. Instead, he went off and had the man thrown into prison until he could pay the debt. When the other servants saw what had happened, they were greatly distressed and went and told their master everything that had happened. Then the master called the servant in. 'You wicked servant.' he said, 'I canceled all that debt of yours because you begged me to. Shouldn't you have had mercy on your fellow servant just as I had on you?' In anger his master turned him over to the jailers to be tortured until he should pay back all he owed. This is how my heavenly Father will treat each of you unless you forgive your brother from your heart.

The Avoider is apt to focus on the importance of being freely forgiven and emphasize entitlement in the forgiveness process. The Avoider may then quickly skip to Luke 6:37,

> Do not judge, and you will not be judged. Do not condemn, and you will not be condemned. Forgive, and you will be forgiven.

The irony in all of this for Avoiders is that in using these scriptures inappropriately, they are really only sabotaging themselves, digging a deeper pit of deception and self-justification, and moving farther away from God's freeing grace.

Forgiveness and Avoiding Change

The Avoider believes that receiving forgiveness from others is his or her right. The injured party should be the focus of forgiveness, but the Avoider makes him or herself the focus. The Avoider expects to receive forgiveness without understanding that forgiveness is given by the injured party to free him or her from the pain resulting from the injury done by the Avoider. Frequently the Avoider simply wants to be absolved from responsibility for his or her actions and willingly accepts forgiveness from others without ever repenting. The forgiveness may be used as a license to continue the old patterns.

Forgiveness is not a helpful gift to give to another if it enables destructive behaviors to continue. God does not forgive us until we repent. He does ask us to forgive others for our own sake, so we are not bound by the evil of another person's actions. God will not forgive us without our sincere desire for life change.

The Avoider seeks forgiveness without sincere confession. We actually harm people if we forgive them for their sake and absolve them from responsibility for their actions.

Manipulation

The Avoider uses manipulation as a tool to press others into his or her service. Manipulation may be forceful and direct as the Avoider pushes others to compel them into compliance. Manipulation may also be subtle and indirect, emphasizing how the Avoider should be pitied and catered to, because after all, his or her needs are most important.

An Avoider will try to sidestep responsibility by attempting to convince others that only God can know his or her heart. He or she may explain that God sees sincerity and a genuine desire for change. However, the Bible directs believers to make judgment calls about people's behaviors. A differentiation should be made between judgment calls and judging. We'll explore that issue more in a later chapter. For now, let's explore this very interesting passage in Ezekiel:

> Son of man, I have made you a watchman for the house of Israel; so hear the word I speak and give them warning from me. When I say to a wicked man, 'You will surely die,' and you do not warn him or speak out to dissuade him from his evil ways in order to save his life, that wicked man will die for his sin, and I will hold you accountable for his blood. But if you do warn the wicked man and he does not turn from his wickedness or from his evil ways, he will die for his sin, but you will have saved yourself. Again, when a righteous man turns from his righteousness and does evil, and I put a stumbling block before him, he will die. Since you did not warn him, he will die for his sin. The righteous things he did will not be remembered, and I will hold YOU accountable for his blood. But if you do warn the righteous man not to sin and he does not sin, he will surely live because he took warning, and you will have saved yourself. (3:17-21.)

This is a harsh passage given to Ezekiel, and its message is important for us. Overlooking or ignoring its consequences is serious business. God will hold us accountable as well if we clearly recognize sin and do nothing about it. We become an accomplice to the Avoider by not confronting sin. Avoiders also excuse their behavior by using passages like 2 Corinthians 5:17-19,

> Therefore, if anyone is in Christ, he is a new creation; the old has gone, the new has come! All this is from God, who reconciled us to himself through Christ and gave us the

ministry of reconciliation: that God was reconciling the world to himself in Christ, not counting men's sins against them. And he has committed to us the message of reconciliation.

The Avoider longs for others to be tricked into believing that for a Christian, every evil or wrong act is now under the cover of our new creation in Christ. Avoiders want others to have no reason to hold them accountable for any past or continuing patterns of behavior or to bring old issues up to them. The major deception in this strategy is to convince others that if they do not believe that the old is gone, Christ's redemptive qualities cannot be trusted. Of course no one would want to maintain that Christ is not able to redeem, so the Avoider's subtle manipulation achieves its goal. Such manipulation is treacherous, because Christians will agree to the redemptive power of Jesus Christ, forgetting that His forgiveness is given *ONLY* to those who seek it and who truly repent. Repentant people are not going to manipulate others with scripture to avoid the reality of who they have been. Repentant people willingly listen to those they have wounded as they expose past wrongs.

Further Distortions of the Avoider

The Avoider may also try to distort reality by quoting passages like Psalm 103:12, "As far as the east is from the west, so far has he removed our transgressions from us." Avoiders often quote these passages when they are resisting recovery and before they repent. When an Avoider repents, he or she recognizes the value of remembering what has been done, so that such conduct might be avoided in the future. Even though this behavior is now in the past, repentant Avoiders learn the value of facing who they were and what they did to others. Realizing how they have wronged others and understanding the consequences of these actions brings profound healing.

Avoiders also may distort the issue of unconditional love (1 Corinthians 13). They like to highlight the idea that love is patient, which they translate as others' need constantly to tolerate and support their resistance to change. Their conception of love translates as "you are never to confront me or share your anger with me." An unfailing love means that "you can never threaten to withdraw yourself emotionally or leave the relationship if I do not change." Lack of pride in love translates to "If you call me on my sin, you are playing God and are proud and haughty." Love keeping no record of wrongs translates to "you are to not to point out destructive and continuing sin to challenge and hold me accountable for my repentance and change."

Reactions of Others

Rarely does the Indulger in false guilt ever take these passages and turn them back toward the Avoider who was meant to hear them. Instead, the Indulger takes too much responsibility for each situation and re-examines his or her own life, totally missing the manipulation just wrought by the Avoider. The Indulger then becomes an accomplice in the sin of the Avoider, with both failing to grow in grace. Love is defined in Romans 12:9 this way: "Let love be sincere; hate what is evil, hold fast to what is good." When we allow ourselves to be manipulated or to manipulate others we lose sight of love.

I'll Blame You, Not Me

The Avoider changes the focus of responsibility from him or herself to others. Each finds ways to make every difficulty or conflict become someone else's responsibility. The more they talk, the more the conversation will inevitably make them the victim of others, and engage people either to pity them or to join them in blaming others for their problems. The sad reality of all this destruction is that the Avoider fails truly to experience God's immense grace through repentance. They not only fail to love others and miss the task of the greatest commandments, but they

Avoiding True Guilt: Running from Grace

also miss out on God's rich and complete forgiveness. God longs to use His power to change our hearts, mold us, and make us in His image.

Another consequence of avoiding true guilt is that the people the Avoider may truly want to love end up being seriously injured and abused through the Avoider's self-centered need for self-protection. All the while, the Avoider is oblivious to this self-deception and lack of love in all of the defenses that he or she becomes blinded to.

> Why do you look at the speck of sawdust in your brother's eye and pay no attention to the plank in your own eye? How can you say to your brother, 'Brother, let me take the speck out of your eye,' when you yourself fail to see the plank in your own eye? You hypocrite, first take the plank out of your eye, and then you will see clearly to remove the speck from your brother's eye. (Luke 6:41-42)

Unfortunately, this passage which is designed to keep people from destructiveness may be used instead to destroy. These verses challenge each of us to accept responsibility for ourselves, and are specifically directed to the Avoider. Christ designed this passage to address Avoiders who very predictably blame others, who believe they have only small issues to consider (as is typically an accurate picture of the Indulger in false guilt), instead of looking at the plank of sin in their own life. God's heart must grieve as He sees the people He loves misusing His precious, beautiful scriptures. Paul outlined consequences for avoiding personal responsibility:

> You, therefore, have no excuse, you who pass judgment on someone else, for at whatever point you judge the other, you are condemning yourself, because you who pass judgment do the same things. Now we know that God's judgment against those who do such things is based on truth. So when you, a mere man, pass judgment on

them and yet do the same things, do you think you will escape God's judgment? (Romans 2:13)

The issue here is hypocrisy. Avoiders of true guilt choose to focus on another in order to avoid self-examination. God's challenge to them through His harshness is to stop running away from who they really are. It is critical for Avoiders of true guilt to focus on the ugliness of their own sin so they can move toward repentance.

> Have nothing to do with the fruitless deeds of darkness, but rather expose them. For it is shameful even to mention what the disobedient do in secret. But everything exposed by the light becomes visible, for it is light that makes everything visible. (Ephesians 5:11-14)

God puts up a mirror to help us see. He gives Avoiders passages to bring their failures to light. God knows it is critical to be honest in self-examination before change can happen, and harshness is the language of light for the Avoider of true guilt. If light is not chosen, judgment cannot be escaped.

Consequences of Sinful Conduct

God wants the Avoider to know that there are consequences for continued sinful patterns. He confronts denial and refusal to hear truth. Matthew 18:15-20, explains that if a man refuses to hear truth, others should tell him individually, next, they should tell him before two or three others, then tell him before the church and if he still does not listen, treat him as a tax collector or pagan. God thus directs the church to repudiate evil behaviors. 1 Corinthians 5:12 describes how the church should expel the wicked Christian.

> Warn a divisive person once, and then warn him a second time. After that, have nothing to do with him. You may be sure that such a man is warped and sinful; he is self-condemned. (Titus 3:10-11)

God uses strong language to describe the Avoider's distortion.

In Mark 3:5 Jesus was angry and deeply distressed by the Pharisees' lack of compassion for the man with the withered hand. God wants us to walk in love and never to use rules to supersede compassion and growth. He longs to have us move out of a self-centered world and He speaks harshly to those who live in self-preoccupation. He knows that the only way to break through such self-centeredness is through tough confrontation by Scripture or by other people.

Harshness and Grace

Because they deceive and manipulate themselves and those around them as they blindly seek to avoid responsibility for their own actions, God deals very harshly with Avoiders. He challenges them to step out of their self-centeredness and confronts their belief that self-sufficiency produces positive outcomes. God must grieve to watch the hurt and abuse that inevitably is transferred to those who most need to know His love.

Superficial Relationships

The Avoider of true guilt is often skilled at first impressions, but is unable to maintain and sustain these impressions. The Avoider cannot handle deeper intimacy where manipulative thinking and actions can no longer be disguised. The Avoider may have numerous superficial relationships that outwardly appear positive because he or she does not have to maintain the good impression on a deeper level. Superficial relationships thrive because the Avoider has people's admiration and respect, even though it is undeserved and actually enables the Avoider further to delay repentance.

Change You Not Me

Avoiders usually will not seek help or go for therapy unless they are likely to lose something they want to keep. Their investment in change is aimed at convincing others that they are "fixed" and everything else should return to old comfort zones and behavior patterns. Avoiders typically will not want anyone intimate with them to have any contact with their therapist if they do enter therapy, because that will allow the intimate support person to expose to the therapist what really is going on. Therapy may also reveal the areas where the Avoider is failing to follow the therapist's recommendations. Contact between the therapist and others in the Avoider's life is necessary for the healing process to begin and continue. An alliance between the therapist and significant others in the Avoider's life is critical for effective therapy as it will enhance the healthy increasing discomfort of the Avoider. If the therapist is competent, the Avoider will predictably try to discredit and demean the therapist and will want to find someone more "competent." Essentially they will quit the confronting therapy and try to find another therapist whose recommendations are comfortable.

Avoiders love the thought of effortless change and work at convincing others of instant miracles. Vague generalities will flow from their mouths rather than details of specific reformations, heart-felt conviction, or altered patterns for the future. The Avoider's problem-solution is based on control and self-will, not on surrendering his or her plan and will to God. Trying harder becomes frustrating and is a path of burnout, because it depends on one's own strength without considering God's power of repentance. It is the Avoider's predictable yet dangerous response.

Hollow Promises

Avoiders will promise that they will never hurt you again or that things will be different next time. They may be able to maintain the change for a short period, but the old pattern of control will resume and they will not be able to maintain long-term change. Signs that the reformed lifestyle will not last are illustrated by the lack of real awareness of the way they have impacted others. In their minds, they have changed and you will be at fault if you do not view their change as genuine and legitimate.

The Avoider of true guilt may display intense self-hatred and shame him or herself. This deceptive tactic is used to prevent others' confronting the problem. Such catch-phrases may be used as, "I hate myself for what I've done to you, I don't know how you could ever love someone as terrible and appalling as I," or "'I feel so much shame and disgust for the horrible, awful things I've done. How can I ever show my face?" The Indulger in false guilt mistakes this self-hatred for the Avoider's repentance. Indulgers feel bad for "making the Avoider hate him or herself," so they back off and do not push for further indications of true repentance. The Avoider uses "feeling horrible themselves" as a way to stay self-focused and self-absorbed. He or she will avoid realizing what pain has been caused when the only person perceived is himself or herself.

When the Avoider chooses to hate him or herself it often short-circuits legitimate pain and anger, because the Indulger's feelings appear only to be "causing" the Avoider to hate the self. Indulgers know that self-bashing is unproductive, so they may actually feel responsible for the Avoider's failure to change in response to the Indulger's sharing honest feelings.

The Self-Pity Pit

Avoiders present a mock version of repentance and "prove" how sorry they are by appearing to hate themselves. Self-hatred however, has nothing to do with repentance. The Avoider can often summon tears to increase dramatic impact; feeling sorry for him or herself and for resulting potential losses. Such tears show no indication of sincere repentance. They can weep bitterly over how cruel people are to them, but the tears don't acknowledge the damage and injury they have done to others. They will often look at you with a blank face when you describe your pain to them, when a few seconds earlier they may have been weeping for themselves. They may even grow angry with you for sharing your pain, although they have no problem crying in self-pity. Their tears are a tool for manipulation rather than an indication of true repentance. Anything other than true remorse keeps the Avoider from experiencing God's power, love and grace.

Making Craziness

The Avoider may try to convince you that you are irrational if you pinpoint what appears to be a non-existent problem, or may argue details with you until the original issue is obscured, lost in a jungle of insignificant trifles. The Avoider may tell you that you have been defensive or unbalanced and do not think logically. The conversation may be prolonged so long that the initial concern is obscured. Through such behaviors as these, Avoiders distract you from their manipulation and may convince you that all difficulties are your own. They may even become so skilled at such manipulation that you begin to discount your own accurate perceptions of reality.

Avoiders will often push others toward self-doubt by encouraging you to mistrust your gut-level feelings. Their constant lying can cause others to mistrust every past or continuing suspicion. The Avoider may try to convince you not to trust your own instincts and to relinquish any ideas for which you do not have tangible evidence.

Further Smokescreens

Avoiders will sidetrack you with your own errors or with insignificant details. They may compare themselves to others who have a more severe and often unrelated problem to convince you that they are just fine. Or they may compare you to others in their own experience who have had incredible patience toward them, and because of this individual's patience and "love" the Avoider was able to "change". They often will tell others that because you have not met their needs, you have caused their problem in the first place and if you were more understanding, caring, and loving, and "tried" harder to understand them, you could be more supportive and not so pushy and controlling. They may emphasize small trifles in which you have failed to love them in the past, using this tactic to increase your sense of guilt, and to remove the focus from themselves.

Avoiders sometimes talk about how they were abused in their childhood. They may glory in stories of the mistreatment to justify their present bitterness, resentment and inappropriately destructive behaviors. They will strive to erect a foundation of sympathy, empathy, and particularly pity for themselves. They bring up their past to justify their inability to control their present conduct. As long as people stay locked into their past, they will never need to change in the present, and this avoidance of change unfortunately is their primary goal. If the Avoider changes, he or she will lose the desire and ability to be destructive in these ugly and deceitful ways.

I'm Perfect—at Least *I* Think I Am

Avoiders may also use scripture passages such as Philippians 3:12-14,

> Not that I have already obtained all this, or have already been made perfect, but I press on to take hold of that for which Christ Jesus took hold of me. Brothers, I do not consider myself yet to have taken hold of it. But one thing I do: Forgetting what is behind and straining toward what is ahead, I press on toward the goal to win the prize for which God has called me heavenward in Christ Jesus.

Interestingly, Avoiders will overlook the next two verses which give a different context to verses 12 and 13 than Avoiders would like to acknowledge.

> All of us who are mature should take such a view of things. And if on some point you think differently, that too God will make clear to you. Only let us live up to what we have already attained. (Philippians 3:15-16)

Repentance is absolutely necessary

Christ's Touch Changes Us

When full repentance is not intended it is unnecessary to forget what is behind. God wants us to learn from our mistakes and to move forward, never forgetting the lessons we learned, or minimizing the hurt of someone who has been wounded by our actions. The Avoider wants the Indulger simply to forget completely. Again, the tragedy here is that Avoiders are only hurting themselves by their distorted view of God and of true healing.

Avoiders accuse others of expecting too much of them, or of demanding their perfection. They will tell you that they will never be able to please you. They will tell you that it is pointless for them to even try with you because you are so critical and disapproving. Indulgers in false guilt, on the other hand, struggle mightily to set limits with others and rarely demand too much, rather expecting too little.

Surprise, I'm Cured!

Avoiders try to prove to you that they *have* changed and have recovered. They may say things like, "If you would only give me a chance to show you how much I've changed," or "I keep trying to listen to you, but you won't give me a chance," or "I really feel bad about what I've done to you." They may try to honeymoon you again. Such a "honeymoon" is deceptive. The Avoider may shower you with gifts and praise you for what an incredible person you are, temporarily giving you the love you long for. However, the honeymoon is maintained only long enough to allow the past manipulation to return in full. The crushing blow comes when you realize their loving care was only temporary. The essence of these manipulations is to trick you into giving the Avoider another chance and to accept a pseudo change as real. Remember again that these predictable patterns will not change, short of repentance.

I'm Not Controlling, You Are

They will also attempt to convince you that you are trying to control them because they know that you see control as a negative issue. If they can convince you that you rather than they are actually the controlling one, you will stop confronting their very real problems. They may try to convince you that you are controlling them by labeling your limits "threats". They may also maintain that you are trying to change them and make them into the perfect person you want them to be, accusing you of giving ultimatums or posing as superior to them. They treat relationships as power plays, and assume that others do the same. Legitimate, balanced control holds Avoiders responsible for themselves and holds you responsible for setting your own appropriate boundaries.

The Intimidator

Avoiders may also try numerous scare tactics such as telling you that they are tired of your critical, hardhearted, cold and distant attitude. They state that they don't need such a negative, pessimistic person in their lives and that they will find someone who will truly understand their good heart and will appreciate them for who they are without trying to change them. They state that they no longer care about you and do not need you anymore. They may threaten to leave or kill themselves if you do not, start being more "loving" to them. They hope that these scare tactics will avert consequences for their actions or will make you become their prime enabler and supporter in their manipulations. As they attempt to intimidate you so that you will not set limits and will fear for your own life, you resign yourself to doing nothing and tolerating their abuse rather than to risk further emotional or physical hurt to yourself.

Avoiders may maintain that they are physically falling apart, with numerous symptoms such as panic attacks, diarrhea, sweats, stomach pains, nausea, increased blood pressure, neck tension, sleepless nights, or migraine headaches. The point of telling you these physical problems is to blame you for causing them. You "caused the symptoms," they tell you, because of your confrontation, your need for their perfection, and your lack of empathy and support for them. They are trying to manipulate you, using these terrible physical problems as evidence that you need to back off and in turn return to enabling them. When they are confronted with their manipulative behaviors, they can no longer control these areas easily. Do not enable them by backing off from the confrontation. Increase your resistance. Their symptoms will then continue to multiply and may help them begin to see their own hyper-control and manipulation. Their physical problems possibly are caused by their need to work harder and harder to try to manipulate other people and situations.

Pseudo Health Revisited

Avoiders of true guilt are also likely to distort healthy concepts such as setting boundaries, being vulnerable, sharing feelings, and being assertive. They mutilate these concepts by choosing to destroy others with them rather than to use them as media for their own growth. Examples of typical Avoider comments are: "I'm choosing to assert my need to make healthy active choices, and I'm choosing not to be threatened by your demand that I go to 12-step meetings, and I am allowing myself to have boundaries and say, 'No.'" "I'm hurt that you keep threatening me. I'm setting a boundary of choosing not to tell anyone the truth of what I've done because it is between me and God. I know I need to be vulnerable so I want you to know that it hurts me when you don't trust me or believe how hard I am working."

Repentance: A Matter of the Heart

Heartfelt repentance is a concept presenting utmost difficulty for the Avoider. The main thrust of the Avoider's tactics in relationships is to ignore God's call to repentance. True contrition comes from deep within the soul, and reflects acceptance of responsibility for one's actions. Repentance brings one to an about-face, to do the opposite from what was done in the past. It produces deep love for those who are wounded. For the Avoider, repentance means doing away with all of the self-protecting mechanisms of the past, and coming to a full acceptance of blame and responsibility before God.

We often see Avoiders approach repentance in yet another attempt to make themselves look good. "Two men went up to the temple to pray, one a Pharisee and the other a tax collector." (Luke 18:10) The clinical term for this approach to repentance is "compliance." The compliant person goes along with treatment plans and completes treatment assignments for the purpose of looking good. These individuals say and do all of the "right things" without really making a commitment to deep personal change. They are model patients, but frequently return to destructive patterns shortly after leaving treatment.

Jesus' message to the Avoider is that superficial repentance is worthless. God is not interested in pomp and circumstance. He eventually will strip away our pride and will humble us. Only when the Avoider approaches God through humble self-examination and open acknowledgment of guilt will God give His full complement of gracious healing.

Christ's Touch Changes Us

Chapter Four
Indulging in False Guilt: Running from Grace

Indulgers in false guilt are hypersensitive to the issue of repentance and spend time and energy focusing on guilt feelings, believing that they must be absolutely absolved by some effort of their own. The Indulger is never comfortable unless all guilt feelings subside. The irony of life for the Indulger is that he or she becomes so caught in focusing on guilt that the guilt feelings are never truly resolved. Indulgers may even experience guilt for things over which they have no control or responsibility. This chapter explores the qualities of the Indulger, showing how he or she remains stuck and overwhelmed in life.

Self Quiz
The following list comprises the main characteristics of the Indulger in false guilt. Check those items which describe your own behavior. Endorsing several of these items raises the question of whether you have issues related to indulging in false guilt.

Indulger Self Quiz

1. Use scripture to heap responsibility on myself for things I cannot control.   YES____ NO____

2. Accept blame for things I have not done in order to keep peace.   YES____ NO____

3. Feel crushed when I am told I may have hurt others; over-exaggerate the problem.   YES____ NO____

Christ's Touch Changes Us

4. Believe that I will never be acceptable to God. YES ✓ NO ___

5. Feel that everyone knows how worthless I am. Feel I am useless. YES ✓ NO ___

6. Assume that I deserve the unfair treatment in my life, and I caused it to happen to me. YES ✓ NO ___

7. Repeatedly ask for others' forgiveness even when I have done nothing hurtful. YES ✓ NO ___

8. Expect myself to be able to "unconditionally" love others despite their destructive behaviors. YES ✓ NO ___

9. Have overwhelming expectations of myself: I need to be perfect. YES ✓ NO ___

10. Chronically compare myself to others and fall conspicuously short. YES ✓ NO ___

11. Accuse myself of not being forgiving when I am angry at others for mistreating me. YES ✓ NO ___

12. Have difficulty accepting empathy and support from friends when I have been hurt. YES ✓ NO ___

13. Put others' needs before my own, even at the cost of my own physical health. YES ✓ NO ___

14. Shame myself excessively when I have made a mistake. YES ✓ NO ___

15. Feel I should and could do more to meet others' expectations of me. YES ✓ NO ___

Indulging in False Guilt: Running from Grace

16. Point out my failures when complimented.   YES ✓ NO ___

17. See my grieving as self-pity.   YES ✓ NO ___

18. Have difficulty saying "No."   YES ✓ NO ___

19. Believe I will never be able to change enough. See myself as a failure before starting.   YES ✓ NO ___

20. Overcompensate for my mistakes.   YES ___ NO ___

A caveat with the Indulger self-quiz should be noted. The Indulger is often so focused on guilt he or she will endorse more items than are actually true in his or her behavior. As with the Avoider, having close friends rate your behavior may provide a more objective view of your true situation.

Self-Blame and Lack of Empowerment

Indulgers in false guilt want to blame themselves for every problem that occurs, any tension that arises, or for others' hurt feelings. A compulsion toward taking responsibility for everything is present.

Peggy walked into the office emotionally numb. She stated she was here to work on control issues. She believed she was bitter, and her bitterness has kept her husband from being able to love her. When in group therapy, she rescued her peers from any sort of tension. She disliked group therapy because it was too confrontive and hurt people. She has spent much of her free time trying to take others' pain away, and was not able to stay focused on herself or how she is feeling. The only feeling she could identify in herself was anger. She focused only on getting rid of her anger in order to please her husband. Peggy had much

45

work to do in the healing process to uncover and acknowledge her own deep hurts, and to allow God's grace to soothe her wounds.

Indulgers will work hard to convince others that they themselves are the problem when difficulties arise in relationships. They want to look at how they are responsible for nearly everything. They have little tolerance for anything that challenges the need to look inside themselves. The process of uncovering deep hurtful feelings will often be seen as dredging up the past and unproductively living forever in it.

Indulgers are drawn to scripture passages about putting the past behind. Unfortunately these scriptures are embraced by them to avoid the issue of valuing themselves as God's precious children. This misuse of scripture is not a helpful process, but rather a quest out of fear, to avoid the truth that God values us as precious.

Indulgers also engage in other self talk that keeps them stuck and overwhelmed: "I'm just feeling sorry for myself." "I hate listening to people who are full of self-pity." The destructive power in these statements is seen in the way Indulgers are sidetracked from dealing with legitimate grief issues in their lives. Again, the avoidance of pain and anger keeps them failing to accept God's cherishing of them that would enable them to love themselves.

Indulgers think or say things like, "I have no right to judge anyone else. I'm not without sin. I just need to look at myself." These notions are supported in Matthew 7:1-5, "Do not judge ... first take the plank out of your own eye..."

While Indulgers endorse these verses, the passages are intended instead to speak to Avoiders who seek to blame others in order to avoid their own responsibility. This classic pattern is typical of Avoiders, and God addressed the Avoider audience with that particular passage. Our hope is that Indulgers would trust their own judgment, and become more assertive in resisting others' sinful behaviors. Instead, Indulgers often look at what's

[Handwritten note at top: make the judgement call + hold others responsible for their actions.]

wrong within themselves rather than hold others responsible for the other's actions. They are not wrong for making judgment calls about others' behaviors. What they often fail to do is to follow up with consequences for the abusive actions of Avoiders.

When Feelings are Absent

Indulgers often are so out of touch with their feelings that they are numb. In the example above, Peggy was numb. They can easily sympathize with others, but they are rarely in touch with their own feelings. They deny any perceptions of loss and feel clueless as to why they feel so miserable. They hate tears, considering them "stupid" or a sign of weakness. They may feel that it is sinful and dishonoring to God to be angry. They have often become so used to being disappointed that they have learned not to expect anything anymore. They walk through life in a haze, just existing, but not living. They empathize with others, but can only feel for themselves when attention is drawn to a failure and how it has damaged others.

I Don't Really Need Anybody

Indulgers see any need for others as a personal weakness and failure on their part. They believe that if they were only more godly they would be able to handle everything with a smile and thankfulness to God. They have false beliefs that Christians need always to show joy, never to complain, never to need help to accomplish a task, and should always feel spiritually alive. When they fail in any of these areas, they believe they are a total disappointment to God and are sure that they would be condemned by anyone who realized that they were not able to handle life alone.

Indulgers' self-sufficient self-talk includes phrases like: "Buck up and go on." "Pick up yourself with your bootstraps." "Let the past be the past." "There's no use in moaning and groaning." "Stop being a baby and get your act together." These slogans become the personal mottoes for the Indulger and drive him or her to do things alone.

Sometimes the pursuit of self-sufficiency is fueled by the belief that I can avoid further hurt if I just do everything on my own. In this situation Indulgers mistakenly give too much credit to past experiences and may ignore positives that others can offer in current relationships. They doubt that God truly cares for them and is really in control, because often they have experienced much hurt and disappointment in their lives.

This Far and No Further

Indulgers have difficulty drawing boundaries in relationships. They often believe they are being mean and cruel because they are setting limits. They are hypersensitive to hurting others, and are not able to differentiate between loving hurt and destructive hurt, which is described in Hebrews 12:5-13. Indulgers end up saying nothing when encountering a trying situation, in order to avert what they perceive as cruelty and they thus fail to hold the Avoider responsible. The end result of this vicious cycle is that the Indulger ends up taking on the responsibility the Avoider has just successfully evaded.

The Indulger does not see discipline as being helpful. When they were cruelly hurt by an inappropriate display of "discipline" they view setting limits as abusive. An example of this distortion of limit-setting is seen in a man who grew up in a physically abusive home where his mother would rage and then take out a belt to leave welts on her children. Now anytime he corrects his own children even calmly, but knowing he is angry with them, he pictures his mother beating him and feels like he has just beaten his own child.

Indulgers will often ruminate after setting limits about how unloving and unfair they were to others even when the boundary is completely appropriate. Their first reaction to any action that protects and values themselves while confronting the inappropriate actions of others is one of deep self-hatred. Indulgers often ask many people if they were cruel in unfair ways by their limits and if even one out of twenty persons questions the restraint set, they will decide that they were wrong to set such boundaries. They often search out people who will tell them that they were wrong and discount any positive feedback.

Every Day a Great Day

Some Indulgers refuse to see reality. They work hard to create a fantasy of a perfect family, and become angry when the fantasy is challenged. They cover over others' abuses and encourage denial by all family members. They may find themselves stating, "Your mother cannot help it. She loves you. I don't want you to bad-mouth your mother. Be a big boy and be understanding." They avoid reality because it shows a clear vision of the damage done. Even when reality is clearly exposed, they may defend and justify the "goodness" of the other person.

Not Just Good but Perfect

It is foreign for the Indulger to embrace a sense of personal preciousness. They have as hard a time as the Avoider does in moving out of their comfort zones. The concept of being valuable is resisted from every angle.

Another Indulger

Ed grew up in a troubled home. His father was emotionally abusive and often slapped him. Ed was constantly pressured to live up to his father's expectations. Good school grades, sports trophies and other accomplishments were met with his father's harsh put-downs about how much better Ed should have done. He demanded that Ed give an accounting of each mistake and stressed how Ed would never amount to anything in life. Ed came to believe his abilities were poor despite his substantial accomplishments. In adulthood Ed never felt he had been successful, and continually reviewed his shortcomings to friends, coworkers, and family. Ed became a perfectionist

> *in later life. He thought if things could only be perfect he could finally satisfy others and himself. Ed was not able to allow anything to be good enough. He would think that it could always be better than it was. He saw himself as lazy and unmotivated because his projects never quite reached his standards.*

Early life experiences strongly influence our basic beliefs about ourselves and others.

God longs to show us that His love for us is not based on our performance.

> He came and preached peace to you who were far away and peace to those who were near. For through him we both have access to the Father by one Spirit. Consequently, you are no longer foreigners and aliens, but fellow citizens with God's people and members of God's household, built on the foundation of the apostles and prophets, with Christ Jesus himself as the chief cornerstone. In him the whole building is joined together and rises to become a holy temple in the Lord. And in him you too are being built together to become a dwelling in which God lives by his Spirit. (Ephesians 2:17-22)

God wants us to know that even when we are far away, He still loves us. The Indulger needs to learn that His love is not dependent on perfection or worthiness. God's love is impelled by grace, not by our performance. He longs for us to know His encompassing love.

Ed was able to progress in counseling when he began to believe God's unfailing love and acceptance. Jesus' message of love is the antidote to the trap of perfectionism. God's reality is that there is no way to be any more or less valuable than you are to Him right now. Even at what you may perceive to be your worst, He loves you. You are no more valuable to Him whether you do great deeds or fail to be perfect. His grace is indeed sufficient, stripping away the need for work to determine worth.

We've Got To Do It This Way

Another strategy common to Indulgers is to try to earn favor in God's eyes through focusing on doing right. The Avoider will often focus on external behavior and rules in order to keep things superficially in order and to impress others. Jesus confronted the hypocrisy in this position (see Matthew 23:13). Indulgers may also focus on rules but for a different purpose. They are striving to assuage guilt feelings by complying perfectly with rules.

When others want them to take care of themselves so they can be kind to themselves, they see this as feeling pressured to perform. Standards of valuing can feel crippling as they can never please or reach the perceived requirements. A sense of rigidity arising from legalistic situations creates a feeling of hopelessness in them and they become overwhelmed.

An extreme example of this indulging strategy is seen in individuals with obsessive compulsive symptoms. Obsessive compulsive people engage in repetitive thoughts and behaviors aimed at increasing their sense of worth and decreasing guilt through perfect compliance with some real or perceived standard. Unlike the Avoider, the Indulger seeks not so much to impress others, but rather somehow to assuage their overwhelming feelings of guilt. These individuals will often say things like, "If only ... when I can do this just right ... but what about ..."

The unfortunate reality for Indulgers is that God is not impressed with our accomplishments. The writer of Ecclesiastes may well have had the Indulger in mind when the conclusion of his observations were summed up as "Fear God and keep his commandments, for this is the whole duty of man." (verse 12:13) Certainly God knew we could never meet all of His expectations when He provided for our graceful redemption through Jesus' death.

God is interested in our personal commitment to Him and not our works. Salvation is by grace alone, "not by works, so that no one can boast." (Ephesians 2:9) Consider how unimpressed God is by our works. Legend holds that the only work of man observable from space is the Great Wall of China and this work is not even noticeable several thousand miles further from earth! The Indulger misses the simple remedy for guilt feelings here when he or she feels compelled to earn favor through accomplishment.

Self-Denial and Martyrdom
Over-responsibility may be seen in the Indulger's reluctance to spend time or money on him- or herself. They will think this is a waste of time and money. Importance is given to others, but is seen as selfish when considered personally. Accepting gifts or generosity from others may be accompanied by such guilt that the Indulger learns to minimize or avoid receiving things from others.

The martyr constantly takes the last crumbs. Martyrs eat whatever was burnt. They deny their own needs and feel pleased with themselves that they are so generous. They see themselves as "turning the other cheek." They are often passively angry and may display indirect behaviors to deal with their complete lack of self. Martyrdom breeds inner resentment.

Severe Punishment
Indulgers in false guilt believe that terrible things should happen to them if they blunder. They choose to lay themselves on the altar to be sacrificed, and believe that their mistakes cannot be atoned for. Simple errors are seen as the "unpardonable sin." They believe they deserve a life of misery if they ever hurt someone, and have great difficulty forgiving themselves. They may have done something years ago and have changed from their ways and chosen a path of repentance, but they are consistently haunted by their failure.

Indulging in False Guilt: Running from Grace

I Deserved It

Indulgers believe that they cause others' abuses. They can find all sorts of reasons to prove that they were the ones who made the abuser hurt them. They may say things like, "I was an unruly child, I deserved to be beaten." "I mouthed off so I deserved the rages." "I was quiet so no one could know that I needed attention." They accept that it is their fault because they could not stop the wounding patterns. Sometimes they blame themselves because there was no one safe to tell and thus they never did anything to expose the abuse.

Inverted Self Interest

Other ways that Indulgers traditionally fight and show their discomfort with absorbing God's abundant love for them is by saying typical and predictable phrases such as: "I'm selfish when I look at myself." "I don't want to be a self centered person." "If I care about myself, I will be just like Avoiders." The problem with that thinking is that two very different issues are present. The Avoider fails to love others, while the Indulger fails to love him or herself. The Indulger will not turn into an Avoider by learning self-love, but will finally achieve the balance that God challenges us to as one of His greatest commandments.

Often Indulgers may have been told they were too needy. Such statements as: "I don't have time for you," "Can't you do anything on your own?" "You constantly need attention," were pounded into their heads. They were made to feel guilt even for legitimate needs. Selfishness is not composed of having needs. God longs for us to come to Him to allow Him to meet our insufficiencies.

Anything You Can Do, I Can Do Worse

The Indulger in false guilt chronically compares him or herself to others and finds himself wanting. Indulgers see someone who handles life better than they do and carry horrible guilt for their inability to function as well. They live in a world of "smarter than" "healthier than" "more spiritual than" and debase themselves for who they are. They never feel content with themselves because in their own estimation they always fall short.

Comparisons support the belief that "If I just try hard enough, maybe I could be valuable, but since I am not that able, I am worthless."

The Worthlessness Trap

The Indulger faces a difficult struggle when dealing with feeling unworthy and undeserving of love. The apostle Paul addressed this issue:

> You see, at just the right time, when we were still powerless, Christ died for the ungodly. Very rarely will anyone die for a righteous man, though for a good man someone might possibly dare to die. But God demonstrates his own love for us in this: While we were still sinners, Christ died for us. Since we have now been justified by his blood, how much more shall we be saved from God's wrath through him! For if, when we were God's enemies, we were reconciled to him through the death of his Son, how much more, having been reconciled, shall we be saved through his life! Not only is this So, but we also rejoice in God through our Lord Jesus Christ, through whom we have now received reconciliation. (Romans 5:6-11)

How wonderful that God longs for Indulgers to know that they don't have to be worthy to be precious to Him! After all, as Christians we are co-heirs to the universe (Romans 8:17). Indulgers invest themselves in down playing the power of this concept, focusing instead on their undeservedness.

Indulgers have often experienced difficulties in early relationships that helped them come to believe they are undeserving and valueless. The Indulger's perspective is that "I am only worthwhile if I am choosing to see how I have fallen short of God's and others' expectations." The Indulger believes that when all of his or her shortcomings are duly noted and repented of, then and only then will that one deserve favor from God and others. This strategy to overcome shortcomings and establish worth represents a black hole leading only to despair and frustration. After all, there is always something else that has been done to disappoint God or others.

Poor Me

Indulgers perceive themselves as victims. Other people seem so powerful, and they feel so weak. They believe they have no power to make choices. They often feel trapped and unable to make healthy choices due to the oppression of others or their history of abuse. They feel powerless next to people who have exerted such control. They give over the power of choice to others in their lives because of the past. Jesus, nevertheless, offered a different perspective:

> So do not be afraid of them. There is nothing concealed that will not be disclosed, or hidden that will not be made known. What I tell you in the dark, speak in the daylight; what is whispered in your ear, proclaim from the housetops. Do not be afraid of those who kill the body but cannot kill the soul. Rather, be afraid of the one who can destroy both soul and body in hell. Are not two sparrows sold for a penny? Yet not one of them will fall to the ground apart from the will of your Father. And even the very hairs of your head are all numbered. So don't be afraid; you are worth more than many sparrows. (Matthew 10:26-31)

Jesus reminds us that sin will be exposed in the end and He encourages the exposure of what is evil. He also encourages loud proclamation of wrongs done and challenges us to speak it from the roofs. He goes on to state how much He values His children.

His reminder is that there is no one or nothing that can be bigger than He is. He longs to carry our fears for us, to help us move out of victimhood.

If I Can Ignore It, It Will Go Away

Indulgers are often afraid to be assertive in expressing opinions or needs because they believe others will respond in anger. Voicing opinions seem self-defeating as they watch the situation become worse. Jesus validated the reality of people who attack and want to rob value from the Indulger.

> But before all this, they will lay hands on you and persecute you. They will deliver you to synagogues and prisons, and you will be brought before kings and governors, and all on account of my name. This will result in your being witnesses to them. But make up your mind not to worry beforehand how you will defend yourselves. For I will give you words and wisdom that none of your adversaries will be able to resist or contradict... By standing firm you will save yourselves. (Luke 21:12-19)

Christ warned Indulgers that in the healing process they will find enemies. Avoiders will hate them because Indulgers who love themselves will no longer tolerate deception or abuse. Indulgers will also begin leaning on Christ for wisdom to endure fears, and they will fight for love. He makes it clear that He will never stop loving. He encourages you to fight against those who do not want you to begin loving yourself. He tells us to fight even if others respond with hatred. This fight is a stand against those who want to strip away dignity and is a process of allowing God and others to give real love, the ultimate battle for the Indulger. Winning this battle is not easy, but it is impossible without a foundation of knowing how incredibly precious and valuable you are and how loved you are by God.

Love Conquers All

Indulgers are often deceived by thinking that Abusers need what they need, tenderness. Indulgers believe that if they are only kind enough, are a better spouse, more understanding, and less critical, the other person would change. They see tenderness as the answer for everyone. They often enable Abusers by trying to believe in them, highlighting their strengths, and ignoring their weaknesses. This approach ignores the Indulger's personal pain while minimizing the Avoider's responsibility.

Infinite Worth Through God's Eyes

God reminds us of our preciousness to Him by describing how long He has loved us:

> The word of the Lord came to me saying, 'before I formed you in the womb I knew you, before you were born I set you apart; I appointed you as a prophet to the nations.' (Jeremiah 1:4-5)

And by describing how long He will love us:

> You whom I have upheld since you were conceived, and have carried since your birth. Even to your old age and gray hairs I am he, I am he who will sustain you. I have made you and I will carry you; I will sustain you and I will rescue you. (Isaiah 46:3-4)

God longs to have His children cling to knowing that there is never a moment that He will ever leave. He sees the infinite worth of His creation and appears to take great pleasure in our lives from conception through death. We are intrinsically valuable and incredibly precious to God.

God knows Avoiders of true guilt will attempt to abuse Indulgers as they struggle to know how precious they are to Him. Passages encourage Indulgers to the fight for love. He will never leave in times of battle:

But we have this treasure in jars of clay to show that this all-surpassing power is from God and not from us. We are hard pressed on every side, but not crushed; perplexed, but not in despair; persecuted but not abandoned; struck down, but not destroyed. We always carry around in our body the death of Jesus, so that the life of Jesus may also be revealed in our body. (2 Corinthians 4:7-10)

God promises to be our sustenance throughout the new battle of fighting for what really matters and will ultimately help you to feel loved.

Are You Confused?
After reading the last two chapters you may be under the impression that you are both an Avoider and an Indulger. While it is true that each of us the has characteristics of both types, one perspective tends to dominate. It is essential to determine what your predominant struggle is because the healing process is radically different for the Indulger and the Avoider. Some people's predominant style comes out based on situations. I may struggle predominantly with indulging in false guilt when I need help, because I do not believe that I deserve to be helped. However, I may struggle predominantly with avoiding true guilt when I have actually done something wrong. To determine which is your predominate style, ask yourself which is harder: to receive love (Indulgers) or to take responsibility for your actions (Avoider). The question to ponder is, "What do I say or do more of?"

It is important not simply to trust your own evaluation of your style. Our hope is that you have heard clearly that both types of people would rather see themselves as the opposite of what they really are. In making the wrong choice, you will stay in your comfort zones, but the problems in your life will remain stagnant or get worse. Get objective feedback from others you can trust—not enablers. Ask yourself, "Do people who really care about my best interests give me feedback that I need to love myself more, or that I am being self-centered?" Which category brings up the most discomfort? Take this issue seriously, because the wrong evaluation can make your Journey through healing an endless vicious cycle without any answers. No one is able to change if he or she really doesn't choose to change. Sabotaging can be a very effective tactic if you want to stay the same. Many people want help "their own way" rather than God's way. Even if you worked harder than you have ever worked, and gave your heart and soul to healing, if you chose the wrong path, it won't work.

Christ's Touch Changes Us

Chapter Five
The Healing Process

Emotional wholeness involves willingness to step out of comfort zones and accept new perspectives. Healing involves increasing one's sensitivity to God's messages in the way He intends. The healing process is facilitated by our willingness to be emotionally vulnerable before God. These general concepts provide a foundation for the more specific elements in the healing process.

The Avoider needs clear direction and confrontation to be redirected to focus on God's issues. The Avoider must face repentance, acknowledging past manipulation, playing the victim, and hiding behind truth, thus accepting personal responsibility and moving from control to surrender, being vulnerable, mending destroyed relationships, and establishing accountability in them. The Indulger needs clear direction through supportive reassurances to be able to move through the healing process. The Indulger must affirm that God is sufficient to cover shortcomings, thereby discovering his or her infinite worth through God's eyes, moving to self-acceptance and love, allowing for neediness, focusing on others to absolve guilt, establishing a support network, and sharing the pain. We will address specific ways that God heals the lives of Avoiders and Indulgers in later chapters.

Stepping into Discomfort

Recognizing that the healing process involves discomfort is the first step toward recovery. Dealing openly with guilt issues is a painful process often met with resistance by those facing the need to change.

You have now been introduced to two predominant character styles and some guidelines to determine your specific struggles. The hard part is choosing to journey into the land of discomfort. We can easily come up with millions of excuses such as, "It is not a good time," "I'm too afraid," "After this crisis ends," "I don't have enough money or resources," and the like. Courage to face discomfort comes through reliance on God.

Successfully stepping into discomfort requires us to depend on God. Proverbs 28:26 states, "He who trusts in himself is a fool, but he who walks in wisdom is kept safe." In our own natural strength, we will choose the areas that keep us comfortable. We will believe we can accomplish any goal that we set our minds to. Galatians 3:3 exposes this folly. It states, "Are you so foolish? Having begun in the spirit, why are you now trying to attain your goal by human effort?" God alone is the only one who can empower us to choose His way rather than our own way.

God gave up Himself on the cross to show us how valuable we are. But interestingly, God wants us to hear that our need to see our powerlessness is not simply an issue for salvation only. God wants us to hear that powerlessness and total reliance on a loving God is the way to grow in His grace. His desire is our dependence on Him. We need to get back to a place of surrender and obedience to a God who does have our best in mind.

I Can Do It?

Some of us choose a path of self-sufficiency. We make ourselves our god. We believe God needs our help to make outcomes happen His way. We believe in phrases—that coincidentally are not found in scripture—such as "God helps those who help themselves." "You have to take the bull by the horns." "If I don't do something, it won't get done." In our self-sufficiency, we think we do not even need God. We forfeit His precious gift of grace when we become our own god. Thus we will never experience the reality of a God who is truly there.

Another issue that impedes healing is assuming that God will honor our unrighteous choices. I may think that as long as I am trying, God owes me the outcome I want. God is willing only to give the outcome He believes is best for us even when it appears to be illogical or beyond our understanding. He asks that we stay focused on righteous choices and allow Him to carry whatever outcome occurs.

The central issue here is basic trust. We think God's ways are crazy or unloving, so we come up with our own plan to achieve the outcome we want. We don't choose to trust God to make things right in the end. Hebrews chapter 11 lists Biblical heroes and the chapter ends with these haunting words that challenge us to trust God:

> These were all commended for their faith, yet none of them received what had been promised. God had planned something better for us so that only together with us would they be made perfect. (Hebrews 11:39-40)

God promises only that His outcomes are best.

False Comfort

Consequences I

Three main consequences of staying in comfort zones occur. First, when we choose to live life on our own, we will at best be living off of momentary highs. The addiction cycle will tell you that although you feel good for a time, the high will necessarily wear off, and your perceived greatness and power will be gone. For Adam and Eve, this was their time of seeing and being aware of their nakedness. They suffered incalculable loss for the momentary pleasure of the fruit. You will feel on a high when you live life as your own god, but your foundation is not firm and it will fall. The high is gone and we are left with the face of reality.

Consequences II

The second main consequence is that our control will hurt others. Our desire to push God away and control life on our own is the central element of the fall of Adam and Eve. Scripture states that the consequences of sins are passed on from generation to generation. This could mean seeing your children unable to love themselves because they saw how little you loved yourself rather than seeing how much you gave to them. Or maybe you will watch your child choose someone who abuses them because you never stood up to the abuser in your own life. Or perhaps you will see your child carry on with a sexual addiction when you had addictions of your own. Or maybe you will watch your child trying to be different and yet getting into an unhealthy extreme with the differences. Perhaps, your child so hated being poor that they live their life exclusively for possessions, believing that money is the answer to happiness. Perhaps the legacy you will leave is encouraging your children to believe they too can attain their goals by their own effort. Our control will never impact ourselves only, for it also impacts others. We would have made the same choice as Eve did and that's why we face the same consequences. We are currently still making Eve choices.

Consequences III

The third main consequence of control is to forfeit growing in the knowledge of grace because <u>grace depends on our trust and faith in God rather than in ourselves</u>. It is a miraculous gift we can never make full sense of:

> Are you so foolish? After beginning with the Spirit, are you now trying to attain your goal by human effort? (Galatians 3:3)

Other potential consequences of controlling patterns include lost relationships through separation or divorce, or terminated friendships. Sometimes consequences manifest themselves in physical symptoms such as headaches, muscle tension, pain, nausea, ulcers or hypertension. Finally consequences can manifest themselves in depression, anxiety, or compulsive patterns (alcoholism, drug addiction, obesity, sexual addiction, gambling addiction, etc.).

Surrendering control allows God to provide true comfort:

> Come to me, all you who are weary and burdened, and I will give you rest. Take my yoke upon you and learn from me, for I am gentle and humble in heart, and you will find rest for your souls. For my yoke is easy and my burden is light. (Matthew 11:28-30)

Psalm 55:22 encourages us to, "Cast your cares on the Lord and he will sustain you; he will never let the righteous fall." He promises in Philippians 4:6-7 that if we give our requests to God, a peace we could never find by ourselves will be there no matter what the outcome. God wants us to allow Him to fashion the outcomes. Powerlessness is our choice to surrender our need to control and determine outcomes, and to allow ourselves to believe that God is in charge of the consequences. Powerlessness is *not* about quitting or giving up, instead it *is* about letting go of our natural preoccupation with controlling outcomes and believing if we just try hard enough, we can prevent the terrible things we don't want to happen. Powerlessness requires that I will live a life of obedience, not focusing on the outcomes, but allowing God to be in charge of all results. I need only to choose the paths of obedience to Him.

When we refuse to surrender, we continue to walk in a path of our comfort zones, and God continues to call us to step out of them. Right after telling us how much He values us, even more than the sparrows, He tries to stress the issue of our need to step out of our familiar ruts to trust fully in Him:

> Whoever acknowledges me before men, I will also acknowledge him before my Father in heaven. But whoever disowns me before men, I will disown him before my Father in heaven. Do not suppose that I have come to being peace to the earth. I did not come to bring peace, but a sword. For I have come to turn 'a man against his father,

a daughter against her mother, a daughter-in-law against her mother-in-law—a man's enemies will be the members of his own household.' Anyone who loves his father or mother more than me is not worthy of me; and anyone who does not take his cross and follow me is not worthy of me. Whoever finds his life will lose it, and whoever loses his life for my sake will find it. (Matthew 10:32-39)

The challenge here is not to betray family, but to be willing to step out of your comfort zones for the sake of Christ and for relinquishing your life so you can gain it. He chose to use relationships that we would not willingly let go of, like those with family, to show us that even when His way does seem logical, it's the only valid path to take. We will never be able to know what there is to gain, until we start letting go of our need to control outcomes, and allow God to be in charge of the final results.

Advantages to living a surrendered life, choosing surrender and stepping out of our comfort zones leads to feeling open, relaxed, grateful, safe, tolerant, peaceful, serene, loved, teachable, willing, and hopeful. Even in trauma there is peace.

> I am not saying this because I am in need, for I have learned to be content whatever the circumstances. I know what it is to be in need, and I know what it is to have plenty. I have learned the secret of being content in any and every situation, whether well-fed or hungry, whether living in plenty or in want. I can do all things through Christ who strengthens me. (Philippians 4:11-13)

Contentment comes through realizing Christ is our strength no matter what happens.

The Big "WHY?"

A significant aspect of surrender is being willing to let go of unanswerable questions such as "Why did it happen?" Healing requires that we freely choose to allow ourselves honestly to share our grief, our anger and pain toward God. We choose to trust in His wisdom that is beyond our understanding, and to allow for some things to remain mysteries. We begin to realize that questions we considered vital are no longer important when we see more clearly the character of God. Job had many questions for God until he came face to face with Him and then the questions became small and immaterial. However, before that revelation, Job had much sorrow and grief and shared it openly and honestly with God. When God revealed Himself, Job realized only that God was bigger than he was and he simply needed to trust in Him. As Job's trusted, God restored the many tragic losses he had suffered.

Mysteries in the Life of Faith

God does not always give us tangible blessings in this life that we can count on as we follow Him. Hebrews 11 highlights the fact that not all of us are going to see tangible promises from God in this life. The challenge of living on this earth is choosing to believe in what we cannot see and being willing to be shown what God wants us to see, whether it comes in pretty or traumatic packages.

Surrender is not a one-time occurrence that fixes your life and gives you constant peace. It is a day-by-day, moment-by-moment process of letting go in order to trust God even when trust does not make sense. We really can experience and know God's peace in one situation and forfeit His peace in the next. He desires that more and more we choose His way and become conformed into the likeness of Him.

Surrender does not take away pain. Many of us will surrender people to God and these people will continue to make hurtful choices that will impact and affect us as well. Some may lose people they love. Grief over a loss is healthy, and surrender never means that we do not or should not feel. Take, for example, Paul and Silas in prison. They sang hymns after having been severely beaten!

> Consider it pure joy, my brothers, whenever you face trials of many kinds, because you know that the testing of your faith develops perseverance. (James 1:2-3)

God works through any and all circumstances, and provides peace in any trial. We need only to reach out to Him.

Real Life Perseverance

Brittany chose to let go of trying to change her critical spouse. Her releasing did not stop him from being critical. She still has significant pain and loss as she faces reality, but she does know that she can lean on God for the courage and strength she needs to set limits so she is not abused. She does know that He will give her the courage to grieve her significant losses in that painful situation. She knows that she can grow herself, even if her husband stays the same, but the loneliness at times is overwhelming and she wishes the situation was not as it is. She also knows that she can do only what God calls her to do to grow herself, and she holds onto promises yet unseen. Brittany is a modern day hero of the faith.

The Advantages of Antiseptic

An antiseptic is a powerful cleansing agent used to fight infections. We present antiseptic as a metaphor for the emotional healing process. Bodily infections require "strong medicine." When antiseptic is applied to an infected wound it works to rid the area of dangerous infectious agents. This process is not without some pain. Confrontation is the antiseptic in the emotional healing process. Confrontation erodes the defenses covering emotional turmoil, exposing the issues to be worked through.

Let's say you have a wonderfully precious child. This child means the world to you. She has just been accidentally scraped and cut on many parts of her body. Left alone, the wounds could become infected and overwhelm your precious child's immune system. However, you learn that cleaning the child's wounds with antiseptic could eliminate infection. What is more beneficial for this precious child, the pain of treatment, or no treatment? All of us would say here that it would be unethical and unloving not to treat the child, and yet when the wounds are not outwardly visible, we have a different standard. We choose not to "hurt" people, when to hurt them temporarily saves a lifetime of far more serious scars. This is our challenge to you to begin to confront emotional wounds. Jeremiah addressed this issue:

> From the least to the greatest, all are greedy for gain; prophets and priests alike, all practice deceit. They dress the wound of my people as though it were not serious. "Peace, peace," they say, when there is no peace. Are they ashamed of their loathsome conduct? No, they have no shame at all; they do not even know how to blush. So they will fall among the fallen; they will be brought down when I punish them, says the Lord. (Jeremiah 6:13-15)

Here God emphasizes the importance of our need to choose to love rather than just to make people "happy." It also makes it clear that God is unhappy with enablers and will allow enablers to suffer consequences of not treating wounds seriously.

Tough Love

> Better is open rebuke than hidden love. The kisses of an enemy may be profuse, but faithful are the wounds of a friend. He who is full loathes honey, but to the hungry even what is bitter tastes sweet. (Proverbs 27:5-7)

This passage exposes the significance and love behind confrontation, and the power behind being harsh to help someone grow. Love that does not confront is not really love at all. We can easily make someone like us by flattery, but if we remember that their personal growth may be threatened when we do not treat their wounds seriously, we will begin to think twice about what we are doing and will actually begin to follow the way Christ teaches. When we begin to see that emotional wounds are as serious or even more serious than physical wounds, we will begin to move toward healing in God's way and begin to help a lost and wounded generation that needs righteousness.

Confront and Defeat Sin

We have the power through God's work within us to turn people away from sin if they choose to hear God's voice. Ezekiel 3:19-21 reveals that if we catch a person sinning and do not do anything, God will hold that one responsible for his or her own sin but we will be an accomplice. If we warn them and they turn from their sin He states we will have "saved ourselves" and they will have escaped death. He does not demand that we change others, only that we warn them.

Scripture also addresses our ability to pull people out of Satan's grasp:

> Those who oppose him he must gently instruct, in the hope that God will grant them repentance leading them to a knowledge of the truth, and that they will come to their senses and escape from the trap of the devil, who has taken them captive to do his will. (2 Timothy 2:25-26)

We may be used of God to save people from Satan's grasp and from sin, yet we hate the thought of confronting anyone. When we understand how confrontation actually helps people change, God will give us a longing to help people by our confronting. We

The Healing Process

can, through calling sin, "sin" and treating it seriously, help to heal others and be an earthly demonstration of how God heals us.

After recognizing the importance of discomfort in the healing process comes exposing comfort zones. A great deal of effort and energy is devoted to keeping comfort zones intact. Fear of pain is a powerful motivator that reinforces our defenses against exposure. We've learned over time, however, that the pain of staying the same is worse than the pain of change. Distorted guilt keeps us from fully experiencing God's grace. We hope you will have the courage to embrace more specific elements in the healing process that fit your character type.

Christ's Touch Changes Us

Chapter Six
Healing for the Avoider

The Avoider needs to develop a hunger for truth to move along the road to healing. As an Avoider, you need to choose to face the reality of your destructive patterns. It is important for you to see that areas which can easily be healthy for Indulgers in false guilt are very deceptive and hurtful for you if you want recovery. An example of this is tears. For Indulgers in false guilt, tears are very healthy. Most people will naturally comfort tears, but most of the time for the Avoider, tears are not about being sorry or truly repentant, but rather are about a self-centered, unhealthy focus. Tears often mourn about the Avoider's losses rather than repenting the damage done to others. Such self-delusion is very dangerous. An Avoider can justify his or her need to feel losses in order to learn to love others, but the reality is that you need to step away from your own self-absorption to begin to become healthy. The self-absorption is what keeps you wanting to avoid change and continuing to abuse others. If your behaviors do not draw you into true other centeredness, it is not true repentance. Repentance is the most important and significant task for the Avoider of true guilt.

Repentance is much more intense than simply saying, "I'm sorry." 2 Corinthians 7:8-11 states,

> Even if I caused you sorrow by my letter, I do not regret it. Though I did regret it—I see that my letter hurt you, but only for a little while—yet now I am happy, not because you were made sorry, but because your sorrow led you to repentance. For you became sorrowful as God intended and so were not harmed in any way by us. Godly sorrow brings repentance that leads to salvation and leaves no regret, but worldly sorrow brings death. See what godly

sorrow has produced in you: what earnestness, what eagerness to clear yourselves, what indignation, what alarm, what longing, what concern, what readiness to see justice done. At every point you have proved yourself to be innocent in the matter.

Let's break down this passage to explore the depth of meaning and fruit God longs for us to have when repentance is evident. First there are two types of sorrow: a sorrow that leads to life, and a sorrow that leads to death. Sorrow that leads to death is filled with some or all of the following components: destroying, rationalizing, excuse making, justifying, blaming, feeling threatened when confronted, self-pitying or focusing on how unfair life has been, focusing on self and lacking genuine connected care for others, apologizing that cannot specifically point out the problem as those who were hurt see it, and being unwilling to face consequences.

Emotional death or relational death is the reality where true repentance is not present. Scripture states that there is no regret following such an admonition. No regret highlights the necessity of accepting pain you have caused and desiring to embrace its reality. You fully accept consequences with no regret, and self-pity is no longer the focus of your life.

Distance From God

Avoiders have a distant relationship with God because their behaviors have distanced them. When repentance comes, the miracle of God's grace is recognized and you will begin to see God in a real and loving light, even in view of the consequences you may be facing. Scripture begins to come alive again, and you will feel like you are hearing God's messages as never before. You will be incredibly awed by God's saving and transforming grace which produces a greater spirituality.

Indignation is produced as you grow to understand the consequences of the wounds you caused to others. Indignation does not allow rationalization to explain away the hurt, but instead encourages the wounded to share their pain and anger with the one responsible. Healing involves listening and connecting emotionally with the damage you have done. You will also support the wounded in seeing the ugliness and wrong you created by not treating them as God's most precious child.

Trampling on Others

Another fruit of sorrow that leads to life is seen as you accept the reality that you have wounded others and still could easily harden your heart and cause them further pain. It is easy to fall back into patterns that keep you desensitized from how deeply your destructive actions hurt others. You will learn to long to have others hold you accountable for your actions, and you will also encourage the wounded never to tolerate further abuse. You will want them to set limits and consequences if the behavior were to return. The repentant Avoider will also encourage the wounded to stay skeptical and to stay aware that hurt could happen again.

Healing for the Avoider involves earnestness to hear the truths of how your own actions wound others. You will begin to want to hear the damage you have done and will no longer tell others to "go on and put the past behind you." You now know that to listen to the wounded is important as is empowers them to feel safe and to grieve the legitimate pain you have caused them. You realize that grieving is not a quick and easy process, but takes time. You will sincerely begin to listen and care about how your behaviors have affected them. You will listen to them, not to get yourself off the hook with others, but because you will realize that they deserve to feel their pain, hear that you were wrong for what you did to them, and that they deserve to be cared for rather than being wounded further.

Healing involves a longing for restored relationship, a second chance to treat the one abused as precious. When given this chance, you as a repentant Avoider develop an intense gratitude toward the one you wounded and honor boundaries established by the wounded person. The concern is not a self-centered one, but a concern for those whom you have wounded. In repentance you will not be so self-protective, but will sincerely want others to care for themselves and feel safe.

Sorrow that leads to life involves a willingness to make amends. This righting of wrongs involves tender listening without minimizing, blaming, or making excuses for the pain and anger your actions have caused. The pain and anger of the wounded is thus legitimized. The wounded person should not be encouraged quickly to go on and to forgive or let the Avoider off the hook. The Avoider should encourage the wounded to talk out their feelings as long as they need to. The repentant Avoider will also encourage the wounded at this point to look for your changed actions as a sign of repentance, not merely words or promises of potential change. You will encourage the wounded to see reality, even if that reality indicates the Avoider is not in a sorrow that leads to life.

Finally, healing involves a readiness to see justice done (2 Corinthians 7:8-11) and a willingness to face any consequences the abused person requires in order to feel safe. This acceptance embraces whatever consequences happen, realizing that they are deserved and are important to help the ones they have wounded feel safe.

Victimization as a Disguise

The Avoider needs to begin to identify the ways he or she plays the victim role. You will need to start identifying key phrases that may be only voices that you will hear in your head: "If only you *(another person in your life)* would change, I'd be fine. You're really sick." "Other people *(fill in the blank with the most powerful person to accuse)* think you are the problem, not me." "You're just too sensitive." "You make such a big deal out of nothing." "Other people never had a problem with me." "I don't need your constant criticism. No wonder I do what I do—who wouldn't?" "You'll never be satisfied with me, so why should I even try? "You just need perfection and I can't be perfect, so just live with it." "What about me? When am I going to matter?" "You are so selfish and demanding. You just can't ever seem to be happy with me." "I don't need all these hassles." "Why don't you try looking at yourself sometime." "You do the same thing to me, so why should I listen to you?" Any type of thinking in this vein prohibits change and you will not be able to move toward repentance and other-centered love.

The problem with these types of thinking patterns is that it keeps the Avoider from even wanting to care about how others are affected by his or her behavior. As an Avoider, you are deceived into believing that others are keeping you from happiness, and that they are the problem.

The origin of this problem lies in the way you think, and your thinking stays with you no matter where you go, so you can either choose to deal with your distorted thinking or to be haunted by the damage it wreaks in its path. Change occurs when you want to let go of deceptive thinking, and when you begin to long really to know how your behaviors have hurt the people you may have wanted very much to love, but have failed miserably to do so.

Exposing the Deception

After you begin to acknowledge the thoughts that go on in your head and see the destructive control in them, you need then to take a next step to tell the truth about your distorted thought patterns. Examples of other distorted thoughts are, "I'll do this, but only to get you off my back and to get you to let me off the hook." "You're a witch, and just out to make me miserable. I hate you." "Yeah, yeah, yeah, I heard you, now you can just shut up." "I'm tired of listening to you, you whining jerk." "I'll make you pay for what you are doing to me, just wait."

Facing Control Issues

Read books and articles on control and controlling patterns in order to gain insights into your own behavior. Avoiders should not read books on codependency, boundaries, forgiving your parents, or dealing with childhood abuse. These books are likely to facilitate your victim stance and encourage you to blame others and to rationalize your destructive control. Focusing on others is for you a deceptive trap that distorts your issues and diverts you from the path of recovery. At this time you can afford to deal only with your own issues of control, for any deviation will cost you precious time and is a futile venture until you are willing to take total responsibility for your actions. After you have surrendered control consistently, you are then safe to explore whether you have indulged in any false guilt issues. You will be able to face such issues honestly only after you have dealt with avoiding true guilt.

Being Honest With Self and Others

Honesty is a critical component of healing for the Avoider. Honesty emphasizes responsibility. Some examples of honesty may include: "I'm blaming you in my head and that's my control. You need to know I'm not thinking of putting you first, which is what you deserve, when I do this. I am likely to continue to hurt you badly if I keep this up." "I'm really thinking destructive thoughts which make me unsafe to you. I'm not likely to change if I keep thinking this way." "I'm really in control in my head. This is not a good sign for you." "I'm not going to tell you what I'm thinking right now because I'm afraid you will believe the lies in my head and be manipulated by my sickness. Neither of us will get the help we need if I do that." "I'm in a bad place right now. Set limits so you can stay in a good place. I want to work to get out of this place and let go of control, but until then, I'm in a bad place."

You need also to choose to be honest with your feelings even if they expose you in a terrible place. The key word here is to "expose" your feelings. You need to choose never to manipulate others with your feelings. Manipulative ways to express your feelings are saying things like, "I'm so angry with you for confronting me. I think you are mean and unfair." This manipulates others because it blames another person for helpful confrontation.

Instead, in this instance to expose your anger would be to say something like, "I'm realizing how unsafe I am right now because I'm angry and want to blame you for my problems. You need to know that my anger indicates my danger to you."

Time to Grow Up

Oh, yeah time! Big time!

Another manipulative pattern is to fly into self-pity and to cry when people confront you. They in turn feel responsible for where you are and this conduct is highly manipulative. To expose this, you can say instead, "My tears and pain represents my self-focus and unwillingness to really choose to hear you. I'm unsafe when I do this." It seems silly to tell people you are in a bad place, but to avoid this is to double the initial problem of secrecy and add to it continued lying and manipulations. You will not be close to recovery unless you choose to reveal this pattern of behavior, even if this catches you in a bad place. You will at least be moving in the direction of recovery by exposing your thinking patterns at a place that challenges you to let go of control.

Interestingly, the Old Testament is filled with challenging the people of God to remember their struggles in the desert as a way to remind them not to act again in ways that dishonor God. They had even designed festivals to have someone read of their disobedience in the past. To this day we still celebrate Passover, which is a remembrance of God's plan of deliverance from Egypt. That story is one filled with disobedience and its consequences together with the rewards of obedience and God's faithfulness. Honest remembrance encourages the Avoider to be responsible for his or her own change.

No More Enabling Allowed

You also need to realize that you will always be able to find people who will gladly enable and rescue you. Such individuals will never be able to help you recover. They are only taking responsibility for you to ease some of their own pain. You have choices about the people with whom you choose to associate. If you really want healing, you will need to share your control inventory, emphasizing your destructiveness and your desperate need for confrontation and accountability to people who are willing to share your journey in helpful ways. Providing others with a list of questions to ask you helps to personalize the accountability process: "Has anyone confronted you on your control and you denied it at the time?" "What did they confront you on?" "How did you respond when you were confronted?" "How do you feel about it now?" "Did you make amends?" "Did you own up to the control?" "Are you sharing with people when you feel unsafe, so they can protect themselves?" "Are you choosing secrecy in any way?" "Have obsessions of using control been playing in your mind, or fantasies of the control?" "What's your plan of action going to be to flee from evil?" "Have you been honest with me?" "How will I know if you followed through with what you said you wanted to do?"

Companions in the Journey

Have several people hold you accountable. These people can encourage positive steps, but confront and hate the evil in your personal relapses. They should encourage you to make amends, take full responsibility, and return to the path of healing after you have fallen. If people are enabling you, you need to take responsibility for your responses. Have you told them the full truth with specifics about what you have done? Have you made them aware that you need confrontation to change and that sympathy makes your problem worse? Are you choosing to be close to people who are active controllers themselves and are in denial so they support your denial? Are you instead choosing friends who have gone through a personal healing process themselves and know about defenses? Answering these important questions can help you determine your level of investment in your healing process.

You need to take a realistic inventory of the type of people you are close to. Are they people who support and encourage the destructive messages we just mentioned? If they do, they will help you only to justify deception. They are not to blame for your not changing, but you are responsible to educate them in your healing process or to make different friends if these are unable to affirm this vital new direction in your life. Do you tell people the truth of what you do to get their empathy and reassurance, and to hear that they love you anyway? Do you long to hear that your situation is okay, and you are not so bad? Or, do you tell people the truth so that they can be "indignant and alarmed" and hold you accountable for your actions, and your need to change? You are responsible for the way you tell people your life story. You are responsible for choosing to associate with people who will hold you accountable for your conduct rather than enable you to continue old patterns of behavior. If you choose associates from the type of people who enable you, and do not encourage them to challenge and confront you and to see the reality of what you have done, you are continuing your patterns of control and you are evading the repentance that God would long for you to embrace.

The Indulger Responds

An interesting detail for Indulgers in false guilt to remember when interacting with an Avoider is that scripture does ask us to make judgment calls about other people's behaviors. Matthew 18:15-20 would never be quoted by an Avoider who wants to continue to avoid:

> If your brother sins against you, go and show him his fault, just between the two of you. If he listens to you, you have won your brother over. But if he will not listen, take one or two others along, so that "every matter may be established by the testimony of two or three witnesses." If he refuses to listen to them, tell it to the church; and if he refuses to listen even to the church, treat him as you would a pagan or a tax collector. I tell you the truth, whatever you bind on earth will be bound in heaven, and what-

ever you loose on earth will be loosed in heaven. Again, I tell you that if two of you on earth agree about anything you ask for, it will be done for you by my Father in heaven. For where two or three are gathered in my name, there am I with them.

Avoiders quote this passage when emphasizing the need for others to forgive them. Many pastors have interpreted verses 18-20 as a reference to prayer, but it appears that the context of this passage emphasizes the need to bind through confronting a person on their sin. God seems only to request that two or three people agree and confront another in His name, and He agrees to bind this action in heaven. Christ very much encourages consequences for those who fail to accept responsibility for their actions. He challenges the person who has been wounded by the Avoider's actions to take corrective and protective action.

Letting Go of the "Yes, Buts"

Listening to others is essential. Rather than working to defend your Avoider position, begin to challenge yourself not always to respond defensively to the other person. Restating what you heard the other person say and acknowledging their feelings aids successful communication. If you feel compelled to argue, give yourself a 24-hour time period before responding to what the other person said. If they are only sharing their pain, you need to choose to listen and care immediately. During the subsequent 24-hour period, you must not dwell on the conversation. If after 24 hours the issue is still important to you, or if you can even remember it, you can plan a time to bring up your thoughts on the situation. If you do not remember it or it ceases to be important after you have listened to the other person's feelings, stop to see how foolish control, counterattacks, and blaming are and how listening helps you come closer to each other.

Wow! I Can Really Hear You

Some examples of reflective listening include the following: "I hear that you are really hurt deeply by how I humiliated you at the party. I caused you to think that I didn't care about you. Is that what you wanted me to hear?" "I hear you feeling trapped and frustrated because you feel that I always have some excuse for what I've done, and you don't see hope for us because of my avoidance and excuses. I hear that you are very sad, and your heart is breaking. Is that what you said?" Reflective listening does not respond or make excuses, it simply shares what you heard another person saying. Monitor yourself to see if you consistently and reflectively listen to the person you have wounded. You also need to work at connecting emotionally with the feelings you are reflecting back to the other person.

No More Hiding

You must also stop believing that hiding the truth protects others when in reality it protects only you. Hiding causes everyone else in your life either to be an accomplice to this lie, or impacted by it. Truth is essential to love. Without truth the life you build is shallow, like the man who builds a house on the sand. Hiding also keeps others feeling crazy, and even when people cannot name the problem, they can often feel it and are definitely impacted by the deceit. Exposing irrational conduct reassures the abused that they are not crazy. Although exposure is painful, it is necessary if a truly loving relationship based on trust and honesty can exist. Relationships cannot survive without trust, and trust is not to be a fantasy but a reality. Needing to restore trust after destroying it is a natural consequence of the true guilt situation. Secrecy abuses others; healing always chooses to expose exactly where you are.

Antiseptic on Faults

Exposing faults enables the healing process to unfold. Writing out an inventory of past behaviors details the history of your wounding behaviors. This means you should actually write out and answer the following questions: When do you become controlling and how do you express it? When did you begin these controlling behaviors? Describe the progression of your control in your life. How have you tried to stop, excuse, rationalize, justify, or minimize the control? Give detailed examples of control. Write out as many as you can remember. Write out the feelings you had before, during, and after your wrong behaviors. How did you feel knowing you had a problem, but still continuing in it? What has made you choose help? How do you feel about yourself and the situations when you need to control? (give at least 3 feelings). How were the following areas of your life affected: family, physical, social life, health, emotions, finances, job, spirituality, legal concerns, and sexuality?

This inventory will provide personal insight and can be a useful diagnostic tool for a trained therapist. The inventory helps your therapist pinpoint your defenses and consider areas you and your therapist need to confront. Your responses reflect how you view your problem, which is invaluable information to help a therapist be aware of areas where you are continuing unhealthy behavior.

No More Manipulating

While exposing your feelings, you need to choose not to use healthy concepts as tools to manipulate others. An example is seen when Avoiders indicate that they need to have boundaries (a healthy concept) so they are no longer going to go to self-help groups because groups do not work for them. This is a destructive choice by the Avoider to stay sick, not to set healthy boundaries. Manipulating people and situations by using healthy concepts incorrectly only moves you in the wrong direction, away from healing.

Be willing to see your own manipulative patterns. Keep an ongoing list of ways you know you currently manipulate, and share it with significant people in your life. Some areas you may currently manipulate are to try to make others feel crazy, paranoid, or irrational for confronting you. Maybe you lie or tell half truths. Perhaps you are skilled at switching the subject anytime you are confronted, or you may counterattack. Whatever your control mechanisms, you are responsible for exposing them. Honest exposure is one of your best choices for recovery.

No More Faking

You need to realize that if your personal changes are not crystal clear to others, you still have much work to do. Others should not have to search to see if you are in a process of healthy recovery. You are responsible to make that clearly evident. Take conscious responsibility for everything you do and think. Choose not to use your past to justify your current wounding of others. If others see danger signs in your conduct, listen to them and take serious heed. Demonstrating change is a lifestyle issue, not a proof issue. You must change and illustrate that change by your actions and speech so that those you have wounded can begin to feel safe with you.

No More Spiritualizing

God will enable you to surrender past patterns of control if you long to release your controlling ways. He will not force you to let go of your control. If you are willing to stop doing things your way, He will immediately, lovingly, and with forgiveness show His presence in your life, but He demands that you choose to do it His way. You are destructive toward your relationship with God when you say things like, "God is not honoring my desire to change. I keep asking God to help me, but He isn't helping me." "God knows my heart is good. It is not for you to judge." You will need to choose to believe that if you release control, God's way is better than your way. You must allow God to control the consequences and accept that the good resulting from your obedience may not be immediately apparent. God wants to be our substitute.

He demands, though, that we continue to make righteous choices and choose to surrender control of our life situations to Him.

When we choose to let go, God then can begin to change the way we think. We can never change our thought patterns on our own. At best we can try hard, but we will eventually find our old ways of thinking coming back, until we come face to face with God and release our control. You yourself will never be able to change your thinking from self-centeredness to other centeredness. Only God can change you in those ways. He demands only that you let go of doing things your way, and He will totally transform your thinking as long as you continue to surrender to Him. He also promises you peace and rest even in the midst of the tumultuous consequences that may come your way. A common assertion we hear from Avoiders in counseling is that they feel better than they ever have in their lives even with more adverse consequences than they ever had experienced before.

No More Control

You need to begin to realize that if you are having physical symptoms such as sleepless nights, panic attacks, diarrhea, sweats, stomach pains, vomiting, increased blood pressure, nausea, tension headaches, or if you are feeling increasingly tense, anxious, cornered, frustrated, angry, panicky, afraid, guilty, ashamed, uncertain, defeated, resentful, empty, and destructive, these may be signs that you are choosing to stay in control. You may be experiencing these symptoms because you are attempting to manipulate a situation that is outside of your control. We have seen clients who say, "I feel panicky and anxious. I didn't sleep at all last night and my stomach is hurting me, are you happy?" The answer is "Yes, I'm glad you are being forced to see the consequences of your attempts to control. If you let go of these manipulations you would begin to feel safe, cared for, relaxed, grateful, open, teachable, willing, honest, hopeful, peaceful, serene, tolerant, full, and loved. I hope you choose to let go of control so you can feel those things. Until then, I hope you keep feeling the consequences of choosing life on your own."

> Consider therefore the kindness and sternness of God: sternness to those who fell, but kindness to you, provided that you continue in his kindness. (Romans 11:22)

No More Ignoring Help

Staying in therapy and actively getting support in a group setting is critical for accountability. There is never a good excuse for not going to a support group meeting, except when a good therapist tells you and your spouse or significant people in your life that you are in a good place. Some destructive reasons not to go to meetings are that the people in those meetings are really sick, and if I hang around them, I may really develop some serious problems, or they may tempt me to adopt some of their destructive behaviors. This rationale is twisted because healing requires humility and openness. You attend meetings and therapy because you need them. You should never go to a meeting to focus on where other people are, but rather to focus on where you are and where you need to be going. If you are focusing on others, it is a very poor recovery sign. If you are in a good place, you are very aware that you need help and you realize that you cannot afford to look at or compare yourself with anyone else. You also realize that no one can tempt you unless you allow them to, and unless you are wanting to go back to old defenses. Whenever you choose to be destructive you are choosing to be unhealthy, are pushing God away, and are hurting those you love.

Another example of a manipulative pattern is trying to convince your spouse that your therapist is not effective in cases like yours. This is an unproductive thing to do. You are only sabotaging your own recovery and continuing to harm those you love. If you want to choose a healthy path, you will immediately enable your spouse to talk with your therapist as often as is necessary. It is critical for the therapist to have an accurate view of reality from your spouse's perspective. Your spouse also needs an accurate view of your progress from your therapist. Strict accountability is essential for healing. You may feel good temporarily while your manipulation is working, but such feelings will not heal you. When you look for a therapist, seek someone who knows issues of addictions well. Addictions therapists specialize in recognizing denial, control, and manipulation patterns. They know that healing happens only when your thinking becomes different. Choose a therapist who will not be trapped into exploring only your childhood issues, but who will also confront you about the ways you are choosing control in the present. Select a therapist who sees the disastrous pit that destructive attitudes and behaviors cause you to fall into, and who is not afraid to be direct and confrontive toward such patterns.

No More Pollyanna

If you have been in recovery, you have surrendered control to God and you and everyone else are aware that God has changed and continues to change your thinking. When you fall back into control patterns, acknowledge fully and specifically what you have done. Admit that it may now be difficult for others to trust you, and that you do not expect them to. Own up to the wrong in what you did. Be willing to listen fully to the pain and anger your relapse has caused to others. The longer you wait to surrender again, the more damage you will do to yourself and those around you. Celebrate when you return to your healthy new patterns again.

Realize that those who have been wounded will often exhibit contradictory attitudes and behaviors toward you. They are not doing it intentionally; it is really their way of testing you to see if it's safe to trust you again. Be patient. Do not focus on what others say that is inappropriate, but absorb what they say that is appropriate to the present situation. Don't argue details with them, but take responsibility for the pain and anger that your actions did provoke. Realize that they are hurting primarily because of the past, not the present. Ask them if they see you continuing to repeat those old destructive patterns currently. Let them feel and connect to the damage your old actions have caused. Always stay in a past tense mentality. They are not angry with who you are now, but who you were. Let them feel this pain. They will in one instant feel very loving and gentle, and may in the next moment turn cold, angry, and distant. Don't be dismayed by this pattern. They will rebuild their trust in you over time as you keep taking responsibility for your own conduct, keep listening, and understanding their mixed and confusing messages. By patient, loving work in caring, their trust will be restored. Persevere and understand the love-hate relationship those you have wounded will feel toward you.

Do not play on their desire to love you. Do not be overly nice to compensate for being a crude and insensitive in the past. When you are uncharacteristically amiable, they may feel that they are betraying you or not reinforcing your changed conduct when they become angry when a present incident provokes painful memories. They need to be allowed to be furious with you. Realize that they will experience a mixture of contradictory feelings and allow them time and opportunity to work through them. Allow others to set the tone for the relationship as it is rebuilt. Never push reconciliation or restoration of good feelings. Such pressure can distort the natural healthy growth of a normal, loving relationship.

King David chose a path that led into more and more deceit (2 Samuel 12:1-13). The story begins with other kings going off to war while David stayed at home. As he filled his mind with sinful mental images, he was led into unplanned transgressions. The question to ask yourself is: "If Nathan the prophet were to come to me, what would he confront me about?" David faced many losses because of his sin, but in the New Testament God called David a man after His own heart. What path will you choose? our hope is that you will move toward the brokenness of David, who realized that he had sinned against the Lord. God can and will use us if we repent of what we've done and choose a new path.

Christ's Touch Changes Us

Chapter Seven
Healing for the Indulger

While God speaks harshly to those who think too highly of themselves, He speaks reassuringly and tenderly to those who have failed to value themselves as they should and experience the love He longs for them to know. He does not confront these wounded ones with harshness, but reaches out to them with encouragement and reassurances of His love. He places tremendous value on each individual. You who experience false guilt need to believe the truth that you are God's most precious and treasured children. He makes clear our incredible worth to Him throughout Scripture. Compassionate love is the needed ingredient to encourage the false-guilt person to "love yourself as you love your neighbor."

Consider some examples of how Christ treats those who fail to love themselves. One story occurs in John 8:1-11:

> But Jesus went to the Mount of Olives. At dawn he appeared again in the temple courts, where all the people gathered around him, and he sat down to teach them. The teachers of the law and the Pharisees brought in a woman caught in adultery. They made her stand before the group and said to Jesus, "Teacher, this woman was caught in the act of adultery. In the Law, Moses commanded us to stone such women. Now what do you say?" They were using this question as a trap, in order to have a basis for accusing him. But he bent down and started to write on the ground with his finger. When they kept on questioning him, he straightened up and said to them, "If any one of you is without sin, let him be the first to throw a stone at her." Again he stooped down and wrote on the ground. At this, those who heard began to go away one at a time, the

older ones first, until only Jesus was left, with the woman still standing there. Jesus straightened up and asked her, "Woman, where are they? Has no one condemned you?" "No one sir," she said. "Then neither do I condemn you," Jesus declared. "Go now and leave your life of sin."

Jesus knew that it was not condemnation the woman needed to leave her destructive patterns, but for her to love herself in the way He loved her. He responded to her with deep compassion and tenderness. His compassionate love to her was more powerful to change the direction of her life than any harsh discipline would have been.

Healing for the Indulger in false guilt is a journey to the center of God's compassion and comfort. Healing involves accepting God's gifts of tenderness, replacing self-condemnation and lack of self-acceptance with God's gifts of mercy and infinite value and self-worth.

Discovering Infinite Worth through God's Eyes

God wants those who do not know how to love themselves to experience His deep and rich love. A basic weakness in the Indulger in false guilt is difficulty with self-acceptance. We will now consider how the Indulger can discover his or her infinite value from God's perspective. Biblical examples of personal value often included women. In many ways in the ancient Jewish culture women were viewed as second class citizens, with a woman even being considered a possession of her husband with no rights as an individual. God made an incredibly powerful statement about the preciousness of His creation and how much He values each individual through these accounts exemplifying women.

God looks beyond the superficial in our lives. Consider the account of the woman at the well, (John 4:442.) Jesus and His disciples had ventured through Samaria on their way to Sychar, and had stopped to rest and drink when Jesus met the woman.

Jews and Samaritans did not accept each other, and Samaritans were generally despised by Jews. It was rare in those days to see Jews and Samaritans in positive conversation, and more strikingly, never did any man speak to a woman in public. Jesus chose to show this outcast that He knew everything about her, including her sins. He, at a point of her apparent worthlessness, offered her the gift of Himself, revealing who He was. He allowed her to know that eternal life was also available for women, gentiles, and sinners.

Jesus simply chose to be loving to the woman and it changed her forever. She went away from this encounter and told everyone she met what had happened to her. She was so altered by the experience that she moved others to experience the same kind of love she felt. Many came to believe that day. What an incredible day of change through the power of Christ's love to one woman!

Our value and worth in God's eyes is illustrated by the parables of the lost sheep (Luke 15:4-7) and lost coin (Luke 15:8-10). In these stories, Jesus showed that each person has such value to God that He would not rest until we are accounted for in our relationship with Him. We are His precious treasures.

God cares for us much more than coins and sheep! Matthew 12:9-13 recounts the story of the man with the withered hand:

> And a man with a shriveled hand was there. Looking for a reason to accuse Jesus, they asked him, "Is it lawful to heal on the Sabbath?" He said to them, "If any of you has a sheep and it falls into a pit on the Sabbath, will you not take hold of it and lift it out? How much more valuable is a man than a sheep! Therefore it is lawful to do good on the Sabbath." Then he said to the man, "Stretch out your hand." So he stretched it out and it was completely restored, just as sound as the other.

Christ cared so much about the man that He was willing to break the Pharisee's interpretation of the fourth commandment. In addition, He was willing to stand up and attempt to redefine the interpretation of the law because a man's infinite value was at stake.

Moving to Self-Acceptance and Love

Knowing our value in God's eyes is the foundation for self-acceptance and love. God wants Indulgers in false guilt to use His love to value ourselves as His precious children. This love allows us to love others fully, as the second commandment admonishes.

When Christ's valuing is lacking, we are unable to see things clearly:

> And this is my prayer: that your love may abound more and more in knowledge and depth of insight, so that you may be able to discern what is best and may be pure and blameless until the day of Christ, filled with the fruit of righteousness that comes through Jesus Christ—to the glory and praise of God. (Philippians 1:9-11)

This passage highlights why it is so hard for Indulgers in false guilt to see reality accurately. The lack of love for one's self blinds one to the deception, abusive treatment, and lack of value received from others. The lack of self love perpetuates codependency in relationships. But God knows that when love is given, vision becomes clearer. Love gives the inspiration needed to set limits and seek true love.

An example of the hidden destructiveness of being unable to love yourself or see God's value is seen in the mother who is constantly giving to charities and is always putting others before herself, but who inside feels totally worthless. She believes she is responsible for others' happiness, and feels like a failure because she can never ensure anyone else's happiness. When her family sees her difficulty and encourages her to take care of herself, she is unable to do so, believing that she is giving sacrificially when she puts everyone else first. She believes that to love herself is a selfish agenda. What she ends up teaching her family in obvious and subtle ways is that everyone else in the world matters except yourself. She believes that she is teaching her children to love themselves, as she is always giving to them. Unfortunately what they see and take in is a different message entirely. Her action message is that to be a good person, you need totally to neglect your own needs and totally give to others instead. She wanted to convey to her kids the need to care for and love themselves as she continued to give priority to their wants and needs, but she really rather conveys that martyrdom is a desirable lifestyle. She becomes dismayed when her children become codependents, following in the footsteps she has modeled so well to them.

First Steps in Self-Love

Healing requires the Indulger in false guilt to begin to treat yourself "as if" you were God's most precious child. This is not saying that the Indulger will believe this or feel this immediately. Actual acceptance of self-worth is the end-product of a long process of healing. Recovery begins with stepping out of one's comfort zone and acting as if you believed such self-worth true. You can begin to determine what you need by considering what you would give a friend. Ask yourself, "How would I treat my best friend, child, etc., if they had this same problem or circumstance?" Treat yourself the same way you would treat a precious friend. The false guilt person is far more likely to be gracious and tolerant to a friend than to him or herself. Ask yourself, "Would I consider my friend selfish, because he had a need?" "Would I encourage her or condemn her if she tried, but made a mistake?" Learning to be self-valuing is accomplished through replacing the self disparaging messages that you tell yourself with the messages you would tell to a friend.

Remember to surround yourself with grace on a daily basis. Choosing to change your mind is never wrong if such change moves you toward healthier behavior. Even if you return to previous self-defeating behaviors, you can do what we call "after-the-fact work." After-the-fact work is doing now what you wish you would have done in an earlier situation, but failed to recognize at the time. As soon as you realize you wish you would have done something differently, go back and redo it the way you wish you would have done it initially. This process will help you to incorporate the new changes. Be aware that feeling responsible for other people's performances can be a pitfall for you.

Take responsibility for what you did not do, but still do what you would have wanted to do. An example of this strategy is seen when you wish you had said "no" to setting up a therapy session for your spouse, but you had said "Yes." When you realize what has happened you can say to your spouse, "I'm sorry I did not realize immediately that I should have told you I would not set up your therapy session, but I now realize that I am not willing to set it up for you. I can see that I took responsibility for something you needed to do yourself. I'm sorry for whatever inconvenience that causes you. I can understand that you might be angry with me. That's okay, but I'm still unwilling to set up the appointment."

Other consequences arise when you are not taking care of yourself and treating yourself as God's most precious child, the way He sees you. Lack of love toward yourself is not noble but is rather a rejection of the life-giving love God wants you to experience. God's heart is saddened when you are unable to absorb His encompassing grace. Giving to others while neglecting to see your own value to God is not an accurate portrayal of "turning the other cheek or giving up of your cloak." Your failure to love yourself is just as serious as the Avoider's failure to love others. If you choose to take this life-changing idea seriously, fight hard to do the following steps. Step out of your comfort zone and move toward true godliness.

Allowing for Neediness

A friend in need is a friend indeed, goes the old saying. It is much easier for the Indulger in false guilt to recognize, acknowledge and meet the needs of a friend than to accept his or her own neediness. Jesus taught that needs are important to Him. God longs to meet our needs, and desires that we accept our own neediness. Jesus spoke of God's desire to meet needs:

> Ask and it will be given to you; seek and you will find; knock and the door will be opened to you. For everyone who asks receives; he who seeks finds; and to him who knocks, the door will be opened. Which of you, if his son asks for bread, will give him a stone? Or if he asks for a fish, will give him a snake? If you, then, though you are evil, know how to give good gifts to your children, how much more will your Father in heaven give good gifts to those who ask him! (Matthew 7:7-11)

The problem arises because most Indulgers in false guilt do not look at what they need, nor are even aware that they need anything. God's care is central to any healthy change. He wants the Indulger to long to have gifts for the self, not to focus on gifts for others in areas that cannot be controlled. When such a one begins to feel God's love, the paradoxical reality is that the Indulger is gaining self-esteem through self-sacrifice. Receiving gifts will feel selfish, but it is actually a self-sacrificial act on the part of such an individual. It is healthy and other centered to begin to long for gifts for yourself. Indulgers can then begin to see their limitations in not being able to change others and can instead focus on the power of change through Christ's love working in new ways in their lives. God challenges the Indulger in false guilt to see that He wants you to be needy. Most Indulgers never allow for neediness. You may appear to be needy, but the need is not a direct neediness for yourself. The neediness is about needing to have answers so that you can be enabled to give more to others. The neediness is not about loving yourself or directly meeting your personal needs. God responds to the ignoring of personal needs by offering grace. Paul addressed the grace of God in 2 Corinthians 12:9-10,

> But he said to me, "My grace is sufficient for you, for my power is made perfect in weakness." Therefore I will boast all the more gladly about my weaknesses, so that Christ's power may rest on me. That is why, for Christ's sake, I delight in weaknesses, in insults, in hardships, in persecutions, in difficulties. For when I am weak, then I am strong.

Many Indulgers are afraid to be needy. You hate neediness because you believe a powerful lie—neediness is dangerous and leaves you vulnerable to abuse or hurt.

The Indulger in false guilt fights neediness to avoid vulnerability. Perhaps past experience with unfulfilled expectations has encouraged this stubborn self-reliance. The difficulty with this fight is that God's gifts are overlooked and emptiness results. Protecting oneself from vulnerability does minimize hurts, but it also denies others the opportunity to help meet needs. There is no shame in being needy, even though the Indulger may feel ashamed of that need. Christ's message tells us that to be needy is to be human. He longs to show us there is safety and comfort when we bring our neediness to Him. He will not drop or abuse us, but will be the strength needed, *if* we allow ourselves to let His grace be sufficient.

Accepting Comfort

Jesus longs for the Indulger in false guilt to be comforted. His comfort is the antidote for the pain and grief of isolation.

> When I said, "My foot is slipping," your love, O Lord, supported me. When anxiety was great within me, your consolation brought joy to my soul. (Psalm 94:18-19)

God knows what Indulgers need most when you are feeling vulnerable. God longs to validate neediness and vulnerability by giving the needed and longed-for comfort, a comfort that can bring joy to the soul.

> As a mother comforts her child, so I will comfort you; you will be comforted over Jerusalem. When you see this, your heart will rejoice and you will flourish like grass; the hand of the Lord will be made known to his servants, but his fury will be shown to his foes. (Isaiah 66:13-14)

God longs to comfort us, and He also is indignant against those who are not affirming His children's preciousness and value. He states in these passages that His hand will be with those who are hurting, not with people who abuse. His central message to each Indulger is that you are His precious child.

God wants to be there in troubled times and He longs to give solace. He knows how essential it is to have a loving comforter. Paul wrote in 2 Corinthians 1:3-7

> Praise be to the God and Father of our Lord Jesus Christ, the Father of compassion and the God of all comfort, who comforts us in all our troubles, so that we can comfort those in any trouble with the comfort we ourselves have received from God. For just as the sufferings of Christ flow over into our lives, so also through Christ our comfort overflows. If we are distressed, it is for your comfort and salvation; if we are comforted, it is for your comfort, which produces in you patient endurance of the same sufferings we suffer. And our hope for you is firm, because we know that just as you share in our sufferings, so also you share in our comfort.

God knows that when consolation is received, a desire arises to transmit to others this comfort flowing from the "Father of compassion and the God of all comfort." Healthy giving to others comes from first allowing God to fill our own needs, not out of a desire to be filled through meeting other's needs.

Stop Focusing on Others

Indulgers often focus on others to avoid the fear of facing the pain of your own isolation and devaluation. You may fear things getting worse, being devoured, or having plans fail with resulting chaos.

> In this you greatly rejoice, though now for a little while you may have to suffer grief in all kinds of trials. These have come so that your faith—of greater worth than gold, which perishes even though refined by fire—may be proved genuine and may result in praise, glory, and honor when Jesus Christ is revealed. (1 Peter 1:6-7)

Christ knows the struggle that some will have in the fight for love. He reassures us that there is a greater reality of "praise, glory, and honor" in heaven. Love is something to fight for even though this struggle can be painful here on earth. Isaiah 43:2-4 states,

> When you pass through the waters, I will be with you; and when you pass through the rivers, they will not sweep over you. When you walk through the fire, you will not be burned; the flames will not set you ablaze. For I am the Lord, your God, the Holy One of Israel, your Savior; I give Egypt for your ransom, Cush and Seba in your stead. Since you are precious and honored in my sight, and because I love you, I will give men in exchange for your life.

God knows the dilemma of pain in love so He reassures us tenderly on these issues. God gently affirms that there is nothing bigger than He is. He longs for our movement toward lives of love, because we are precious and honored in His sight. He loves us!

God Will Never Reject Me

Indulgers may also focus on others to avoid being rejected: "If I state my needs and they are not taken seriously, I will be devastated." God here offers abundant affirmation:

> Can a mother forget the baby at her breast and have no compassion on the child she has borne? Though she may

forget, I will not forget you! See, I have engraved you on the palms of my hands; your walls are ever before me. Your sons hasten back, and those who laid you waste depart from you ... As surely as I live, declares the Lord, you will wear them all as ornaments; you will put them on, like a bride. (Isaiah 49:15-18)

Here the Lord tenderly addresses the issue of rejection. He illustrates the example with an important person in most people's lives—mother—to show how deeply He understands each agony. The intimate picture of a mother nursing her child and casting that child away illustrates the pain of rejection. God affirms to us again that He will not reject us. He will never forget us. He reassures us that we have such great value that it will be proudly displayed as a "bridal ornament."

The essential step in healing for Indulgers is to stop focusing on others. The only person God ultimately holds responsible for change is each individual person. No matter how hard you work, you cannot change anyone else. Focusing on others promotes the imbalance of love in the wrong places. God longs for us to love ourselves as He loves us. Until you achieve the balance of loving yourself as much as you love your neighbor, you will not be able accurately to love as God calls us to love.

Setting Healthy Boundaries

Another step in the healing process involves balancing change in the area of manipulation and boundaries. Setting up stable boundaries is essential to choosing health when others attempt to manipulate us. Often, Indulgers will try to prevent others from manipulating rather than to focus on what may be controlled in his or her own behavior. Healthy boundaries are set first by asking "what do I need to do in this situation? What will keep me from being abused by this person's manipulation?" Resisting others' attempts to belittle your value and worth will help you focus on your place as God's precious child.

Healthy boundaries are not based on anger, revenge, exhaustion, or rejection of another. Healthy boundaries instead reflect an investment in treating yourself preciously. Boundaries also allow for the Avoider to experience the natural consequences of his or her destructiveness. Wait until you know you care about the person who has hurt you and that the upcoming consequences illustrate your desire for them to embrace grace if they choose to have ears to hear and eyes to see what they have done. Letting others experience consequences for their own choices can be wrenching. Love empowers far more than anger, revenge, exhaustion, or giving up. Allowing consequences promotes growth, and builds strength in character. The courageous setting of boundaries allows for personal growth for both the Indulger and the Avoider and encourages the Avoider of true guilt to allow God an opportunity to change his or her heart.

Minimizing consequences by not setting clear boundaries enables someone else to stay unhealthy. Allow yourself to be angry and hurt when sin touches your life or the lives of others. Use these emotions as motivators to set boundaries against such actions and not to seek revenge. Keep reviewing the behaviors exhibited by Avoiders of true guilt. These people do not benefit from being enabled. They will only continue manipulating and avoiding consequences for their behavior. Avoiders will often ask to be absolved for their hurtful behaviors, and Indulgers are quick to forgive. Indulgers must remember that forgiveness happens slowly, and is never to be offered to help the Avoider continue to avoid.

Managing Responsibility

Enabling is fueled by a desire to care for others. When loving others is a symptom of avoiding yourself, you are at a high risk to enable. One sad consequence of enabling is the loss of love and care so badly needed by the false guilt Indulger. Even if enabling comforts and satisfies the other person it is motivated more by using them to avoid personal pain than it is by true other centeredness. The love that enables Avoiders to continue avoiding is not godly. It is not God's way. If you are prone to neglect yourself, God pushes you to love yourself before you try to love others. If we cannot receive His love freely we are not able freely to give His love. These are hard and painful words especially if you have felt rewarded by your care for others. Caring for others is only half of the issue, neglecting yourself is the more profound other half. Consider how you have approached this book so far. You are likely to fall into the trap of enabling and not dealing with your own needs if you have been more interested in how you could be more effective with all the Avoiders in your life; or in how you could encourage all your Indulger friends to grow. The perspective which produces growth focuses on how you can learn to grow by choosing God centered love for you yourself. God's grace involves valuing yourself and others. God's grace allows you to know how irreplaceable and precious you are to Him.

New Health in Old Friendships

Consider a situation where you have chronically failed to set boundaries and have given your friend everything he or she has always wanted. You then decide you need to start being healthier and begin to set some boundaries. You tell your friend "No!" At this point Satan starts setting the trap. Your friend becomes angry with you and you may berate yourself for the reality of her anger. Satan will fight especially hard as we step out of our comfort zones. He starts by tempting you in your head to believe that you are not a real friend. You try to tell yourself the truth at this point, and the battle begins. Maybe you tell yourself, "I was not selfish to say, "No." But Satan comes at you, taunting you with the lie, "You didn't care about your brother in need." He often twists scriptures to his advantage just as he did with Christ in the wilderness. So you keep playing out the battle back and forth in your mind, trying to cling to the truth, but Satan fights hardest at such times. He knows where you are weak and takes advantage of those places to keep you from truly loving. The battle continues and Satan says, "You are selfish and self-centered. All you care about is yourself. Your friend will probably be a mess now, and it will all be your fault. I hope you can live with yourself. You are a poor excuse for a friend." The truth says, "I'm just holding my friend responsible for what she can do for herself. I said what I did out of love for both of us." But more often than not, the lie seems far stronger than the truth. It never really is, but the battle at this point becomes a losing one for most of us. We tell ourselves God's truth and feel even more guilt because we seemingly cannot believe or trust God. Thus we end up not only with the original false guilt, but also with the added pressure of feeling terrible that we know what the truth is, but are so bad that we cannot even seem to take in or believe it.

Refusing False Guilt

An essential tool in the healing process involves fighting off guilt that is not deserved. Satan tries to trap the Indulger into believing lies that interfere with God's message of personal love. Love is the opposite of Satan. Satan obstinately works to make us believe his lies and to transform our false guilt into self-hatred and feelings of failure. If we believe these lies, we will not recognize the needed areas of healing and will continue as victims of Satan's game.

Let's explore other strategies for defeating Satan. These strategies are based on the idea that Satan will never be convinced by truth. He is bent to destroy us, no matter what the cost may be. The person who benefits from truth is me, and convincing myself of truth is the basis for winning!

Defocusing Tools

Here's a way to stop the battle from defeating us twice. Do not try to control Satan's lies because the lie may become stronger. If you fight lies with truth at this point, you play into Satan's hand, and often make the problem worse. Instead of trying to go from the lie to the truth, stick a Kleenex™ up your nose.

Healing for the Indulger

Yes, stick a Kleenex™ up your nose! The point of this zany strategy is to help you focus on a neutral issue. Humor is a great neutralizer, which is why you should stick a Kleenex™ up your nose. Humorous or silly activities work well to help us defocus. You will see how silly you look, and laugh so hard that you will lose sight of your false guilt.

Other good neutralizers are grandchildren, nieces and nephews, favorite books or songs, hobbies, vacations, or favorite memories. Christian music may be especially soothing for believers. With practice you can learn to defocus and go to this mental neutral at will. The trick is to lose your intense focus on self and instead invest your energies in the neutral or diversionary topic. As soon as you are not thinking about your guilt, it has no power to control you. From neutral you are empowered to go to the truth. If when you go to the truth, the lie returns, you need to go back to mental neutral again, so that Satan does not succeed in defeating you. You are responsible for defocusing anytime your guilt comes back. Do not give up, for victory will result in the long run. While this strategy may initially seem like avoidance of real problems, it actually helps you to avoid getting stuck in the lies, a principle that Scripture calls fleeing from evil.

Defocusing with neutral issues is essential. Subjects which have no guilt associated with them are the ones to choose. Poor topics to select at these times are deep faith issues because many Indulgers in false guilt believe they are not doing enough for God and are considered a failure to Him. One's own children are also a difficult issue to defocus with. When thinking about their children parents often can see things they wish they had done differently, and negative self-recrimination returns. You will need to choose completely neutral topics. Consult friends for ideas about neutral topics for you if you wish to.

Defocusing is a strategy also taught to persons with obsessive compulsive disorder (OCD). A hallmark of OCD is recurring thoughts, which in the extreme may include morbid or grotesque ideas. These thoughts are often disturbing to the individual think-

Christ's Touch Changes Us

ing them, seeming overwhelming and uncontrollable. The first order of business in teaching defocusing is to establish that the thoughts may never be totally controlled, but rather they may be managed and redirected. Second, when the negative thought comes the person says "stop" (aloud at first, and with practice silently to oneself), and begins thinking about a neutral idea.

Other defocusing techniques are called behavioral adversive techniques in counseling and therapy literature. Adversive is what is typically known as punishment. For example, a person wears a loose rubber band around the wrist which is lightly snapped whenever negative thoughts come. The goal of this strategy is to learn the association between negative thoughts, the painful rubber band snap, and going to neutral. While the behavioral aversive techniques are helpful, their use is recommended under the supervision of a trained professional.

I CAN Feel

Accepting and acknowledging your feelings is part of taking responsibility for what you may legitimately control. Because of your desire for self-protection, most of your feelings are likely to be disguised. You may be able to recognize feelings when others are discovering insights about their own lives. This situation represents a mental strategy where you may release feelings and not have to identify them as being yours. This indirect and unhealthy way to deal with your own emotions allows for emotional release without the risk of intimacy. You need to be willing to risk intimacy to begin to become healthy. A classic destructive pattern some Indulgers get into is when they do choose to feel, the feelings are composed of anger at themselves. They may choose to feel how depressed they feel that they have never been good enough to change an Avoider of true guilt. Legitimate feelings are not feelings of self-hatred. Your legitimate feelings will likely include anger and hurt from being wounded by others. This is not self-pity. Acknowledging these feelings is facing reality and allowing yourself to experience valid and legitimate feelings any-

let my hurt & anger from Dawn be feelings that I know are legitimate.

Healing for the Indulger

one would feel who had been similarly hurt and wounded. Bottled-up feelings produce energy and releasing that energy by empathizing with others only releases part of your own energy without solving the ongoing problem. You need to begin to realize that <u>you may legitimately feel and express your own feelings.</u> Ask yourself why you feel pain and/or anger when hearing another's difficulties and begin instead to see <u>your need to grieve and work through your own feelings.</u>

Another strategy to use is writing a "no send" letter to the person who has hurt you. <u>The goal of this experience is to experience the full range of feelings you may have covered up over considerable time.</u> This process may be best facilitated by a trained counselor. The following are examples of helpful letters. These letters represent the painful, but courageous journey to legitimize feelings.

Letter 1

Mother: *no send letter*

I cannot call you dear, I am so angry with you. You wanted all the honor belonging to a devoted mother, but all I got was your anger and wrath. I thought until just recently that I was to blame. I thought I was never good enough. I thought I was worthless because I never could please you. No one could ever please you. I now am starting to direct my anger where it belongs—at YOU. You disgust me. You chose to use an innocent little child who longed to adore you, and rather than use that adoration for health, you chose to instead strip away my sense of dignity. You constantly scared me by your rages. Instead of getting hugs, "I love yous", and bedtime stories, I got to hide in my closet hoping you would leave me alone. You were so wrong to do that to me. I am precious; you treated me like dirt. I am caring. You called me an ingrate. You said I was too needy when I just needed normal attention. You were and are the abnormal one. I will no longer believe your horrible lies about me. Until you can clearly show me you have changed and repented, I will not give you the adoration I would love to give you. I will believe no more lies.

Letter 2

Mr. Rapist:

I used to call you Carl, but I know who you really are now. You are a rapist. I faulted myself for being too seductive. I bought the lie that it takes "two to tango." It took one sick man who chose to violate me. You are a sick man for not honoring my "No." I will always hate that you told others I gave in to you. You forced me, you evil, selfish, self-centered man. I want you to know that the God I serve puts a higher punishment on those who sin against the body. You sinned against my body. I refuse to live my life seeing myself as dirty and disgusting. What you did to me was dirty and disgusting. It angers me that at least temporarily, you walk away like a hero when I pay the consequences. I refuse not to see myself as a virgin. You stole my purity, I did not give it to you. I will not continue to let what you did to me control my life. I am fighting lies, and putting my anger where it belongs. I know that my God will judge you for what you did to me and in that I will rest. He sees me as a priceless bride. Even though you did not value me, I know I am precious now. I bid you good-bye. In the words of King David in Psalms 69 "May you be blotted out of the book of life."

These letters reflect courageous outpouring of pain and anguish. They highlight the courage to begin to express woundedness, allowing God's love to begin to heal.

Healing for the Indulger

Managing includes living with painful emotions. Indulgers have limited willingness to stay with their pain. After a short time, distorted thinking such as "you're a crybaby, stop whining," or "you are just feeling sorry for yourself," comes in and takes over. You are not wimpy, irresponsible, self-pitying, or dredging up the past by sharing legitimate pain and anger. Legitimate needs are not being met in your life, and your feelings are normal responses to those situations. You need increasingly to tolerate your feelings. Elaborate on the pain and anger. Attempt to endure the pain. You are not a burden or a bother to others when you stay with your pain. Once you are able to endure your pain and anger in an ongoing fashion, and can allow others to comfort and care about your pain, you have completed over half of the battle toward wholeness.

You need to begin to realize that your feelings are manageable. You can choose when and where to feel. You need to take responsibility to choose safe people, safe places, and safe times to feel. You do not have to express your feelings any and every time you feel them. You will naturally want only to feel when you are alone. But you can choose to feel any time you want to. The trick is choosing to take the risk. Some people say that they can only feel at "certain times." With effort and practice you can feel anytime you allow yourself to do so. If you are not able to have someone with you when you feel, which is a concern, make sure you journal what you were feeling and then choose to share your journal in the first available situation. Feelings are not a hit or miss situation. You do have the ability to put feelings on hold until you can share them with others. You can always get in touch with feelings that are there, if you want to and if you are willing to take the necessary risk of vulnerability.

Establishing a Support Network—Sharing Pain

Another way you may be feeling your own feelings without knowing it is by crying in movies or when you are alone. Movies can be seen as very safe, but they avoid a healing way to let your own emotions out. Other places people feel, but do not take responsibility for their feelings is in church. No one will stop the service to comfort you, because the focus is on worshipping Christ. By the end of the service, your emotions are gone, and you may avoid whatever it was in your life that triggered the initial emotion. If someone saw the tears, you can spiritualize it as "God working in my life" and avoid the intimacy of sharing the situation with a friend. Healing will happen as you are willing to take responsibility to share your emotions with others.

Change will require you to reach out to others for help, that they may hold you accountable. These friends will provide needed perspective, helping you learn when a situation is not true guilt and when it is clearly a false guilt situation. They will need to confront your perspective and help you to focus on your value and worth in God's eyes. Supporters need to talk to you about anything but the guilt-oriented topics. They can remind you that if you continue to talk about false guilt, you need to snap your rubber band, or stick a Kleenex™ up your nose. If you continue to obsess, they must choose to not listen to you, to confront you on your refusal to do your part, or to walk away if necessary.

You may be wondering why is it so critical to have people to share your emotions with. Indulgers in false guilt classically have been all alone when painful traumas occurred and there was no one to talk to. Perhaps no one would listen, perhaps no one was safe, perhaps you were just too afraid to take the risk. Possessing eternal strength and never seeming to need others only continues the pain. Chronically giving, but never seeming to crack or have normal needs continues the loneliness. The lack of neediness is not a sign of strength, but rather is a destructive strategy designed to keep others from knowing about your hurts and emotional pain.

Essentially, others must comfort you to break the pattern of your believing it is always necessary for you to take care of yourself. God never planned for you to be alone in your pain. He calls us to have a "time to mourn." To continue to be alone with your pain is to continue a pattern that has been hurtful to you and never has helped you to release the pain. Talking out your pain with someone who cares helps you to feel important, cared for, and allows you eventually to step away from the trauma.

Safe people to call on for comfort are typically other Indulgers, or Avoiders of true guilt who are in recovery. If Indulgers are ministering to you, do not focus on taking care of them or curing them of their false guilt, but simply allow their strength to comfort and minister to you. You are not responsible for another's unhealthy choices, but you are responsible to care for your own legitimate needs. As both of you become healthier, you will have a special mutual relationship. You can begin your health by allowing others to comfort you regardless of their personal needs.

A useful strategy in early healing is not to allow yourself to cry alone. This forces you to risk vulnerability and to allow others to care about your legitimate pain and anger. You will need to learn that you are not being selfish, self-centered, grandiose, or unhealthy dependent if you need others. This vulnerability is critical to your health and recovery. You are as valuable to others as others are to you. When you do not live by this standard, you are in violation of the most important commandment which is to "Love your neighbor as yourself." You need to treat yourself as God's precious child, because that is how He sees you and that is what you truly are. You move away from God's best for you when you and others do not live as God's precious children.

Accountability may come from support groups, not just from individual friends. You need support from people who understand the manipulations of Avoiders of true guilt. You will never be able to fight this battle on your own. You will need to talk to people who will support you and listen to you. Groups similar in structure to Al-anon, Codependency Anonymous, or Adult Children Of Alcoholics can be very helpful.

Roadblocks to Recovery

Recovery is initially very scary, for it threatens to change the familiar. One thinking pattern to watch out for is the "Yes but" mentality. This mindset shirks responsibility and automatically discounts the possibility of change for yourself. A classic "yes but" is when the client says, "I know that this is what I should do, but the timing is really off." "I know I should go back to school, but there's so much else I need to do first." "Yes buts" serve as elaborate justifications and they keep you from moving forward. They also impede your ability and willingness to listen to another person, because you are focusing more on your avoidance response than on your real need for change.

Another thinking pattern that can divert positive actions is "What if" thinking. "What ifs" cause undue pressure and stress for the moment, and can mislead you to believe you can change another person if you just plot and plan enough. Such thinking entices you to attempt to project and predict the future. To worry and try to fix areas that are out of your control is crazy and unproductive. We need to focus on what we can do to change ourselves in the now. The 12-step recovery program encourages us to take one day at a time and concentrate on actions that we can truly take, in and by ourselves. Scripture agrees and states that tomorrow has enough of its own worries.

Other problematic thinking patterns include "should" and "must." Such thoughts can cause you to believe that if you had only done something different, things would be better and/or changed. An important principle to remember is the post-facto procedure. It states that every mistake is an opportunity to go back and do what you wish you would have done the first time. You can always go back and change, but be careful of the Messiah complex which states, "If I say it right, you will be healed." Watch "should's" with others too, as they get you moralizing rather than allowing others to choose and allowing consequences for their choices.

Keep On Keeping On

The final element critical to successful recovery is perseverance. Change does not happen quickly, and losing hope can easily occur. Begin to see that changes are for your good and for your growth and they may not be immediately apparent. The true mark of change is your increasing ability to see yourself as God's precious child.

Change is scary, but is also a way to know God's immense and awesome grace. It brings with it freedom and the ability to know love in deeper and richer ways. Indulgers in false guilt walk around with a symbolic crushed leg, expecting themselves immediately to be able to walk again. In the process of walking too soon, you will fall down. Falling does not mean you are a failure or that you will never walk again. Apply just enough pressure to increase your strength and build your emotional muscles. But, be careful not to apply too much pressure, or you can do more emotional damage. Be gracious, patient, and tender with yourself as you journey to emotional healing.

Christ's Touch Changes Us

Chapter Eight
Talking to Family Members

Family members play a critical role in the healing process for both the Avoider and the Indulger. Because destruction in relationship happens to those who are closest, family members are most often hurt by the consequences of avoiding and indulging. Family members benefit from the individual's healing process by fostering grace and change in their own lives. In this chapter, we provide direction to family members of the Avoider and the Indulger. Our hope is to encourage family members to provide vital support by being careful not to judge, by acknowledging their own pain, by avoiding the trap of enabling, by confronting the Avoider and by encouraging the Indulger. Avoiders and Indulgers may also help their own healing process by understanding how their family members may be working to further their own individual recovery.

No Finger Pointing Allowed

Judging does not advance the healing process. It is very difficult to identify shortcomings in others without appearing judgmental. This fact places family members in a difficult position when dealing both with Avoiders and Indulgers. It is helpful to approach a person whom you suspect is either an Avoider or Indulger from the position of having identified these characteristics in your own life. It is hoped that this self-examination process has been fostered by earlier chapters in this book. Acknowledging your own shortcomings allows you to bring humility into the ongoing process of dealing with the Avoider or Indulger.

I (Karen) often tell Avoiders that I know how easy it is to be self-centered because I've been there. I also know the pressure, frustration, and imprisonment resulting from unrepentance. I relate my hope they will choose to break out of their prison and find the freedom, grace, and knowledge to love better as they choose the path of repentance.

Judging others for their actions often results from experiencing hurts and disappointments in the relationship. It is important to deal openly with your pain and to accept the limitations of the healing process. Caring enough to be an antiseptic and to call behaviors sinful is a gift of love.

Acknowledging Your Own Pain

In an earlier chapter, we discussed some of the painful consequences or relationship costs for the Avoider's and Indulger's behavior. One method for assessing this is to list the personal costs you have endured through living with an Avoider or Indulger. Some destructive consequences we have observed for Indulgers include turning others away in relationships, modeling martyrdom for children, enabling sin in others, and teaching children to "do as I say, not as I do." Consequences for the Avoider include family members feeling unloved, not listened to, uncared for, and controlled. Children are taught patterns of irresponsibility, and that the ends justifies the means.

Several attempts may be needed to compile a more detailed list of your personal costs. Such a list is useful in several ways. First, it will give you a strong sense of the extent of costs you have endured. This is especially important when responding to the Avoider who is good at minimizing the negative. The second benefit of listing your costs is that it allows you to pray more specifically for healing in your particular areas of life and in the life of the other person. Finally, your list can provide a starting point for reconciliation in the relationship. We should be clear that in making a list we do not intend for you to charge or convict the other person, but rather to describe reality from your perspective. The list will also help you examine yourself and the steps you are taking for your own personal recovery.

You also need to choose to allow people to comfort you and to choose to share your feelings of pain and anger to outside supports. You will begin to be in a good place when you can allow others fairly consistently to listen, to care, and to comfort your legitimate pain and anger. This is not about complaining or blaming, it is about facing reality, and grieving reality with those who can listen and comfort. You need to choose to be around people who also are willing to hold the Avoider accountable. Others will only enable the Avoider and blame you for not being understanding, not giving the Avoider a Chance, or accuse you of dirty, cruel attacks. You cannot change by logic those who want to enable. Do not invest your time and energy into attempting to change those people. Rather invest time and energy into getting your own legitimate needs met. Expect those who enable the Avoider to find you the enemy. Be prepared for this, and get supports who believe you are doing the right thing. Instead of trying to change enablers, abandon this vain pursuit and realize that enablers must bear responsibility for choosing to be an accomplice with the Avoider. Proverbs states over and over again to not try to argue or convince a fool. They do not care to hear. Proverbs encourages us to disengage.

It is important to realize that you are not betraying the Avoider by choosing to talk to others. Choosing to talk to others who can listen uncritically has the potential of saving a marriage rather than destroying the marriage. Games and manipulation are the things that will destroy the marriage, while stepping away from the games and deception may strengthen or save it. You then have a responsibility to look outside the Avoider for support. When you go to others, it gives the Avoider a strong signal that he or she can no longer escape responsibility toward you and will need really to change if they want to maintain relationship with you. The Avoider will know that others will be able to give you the comfort and support that his or her manipulativeness does not allow him or her to give you. A caution here is to never allow opposite-sex people to be the ones you get support from and share with. You are in a very vulnerable place and need to be responsible for making healthy uncomplicating choices.

Not Getting Trapped by an Avoider

You will also need to choose to live outside of your hope for change in the Avoider so you can clearly see the true reality of the situation. It is great to want and hope that the Avoider will change, but when your hope distorts your accurate perception of what is currently happening, it becomes enabling and harmful. Remember that anyone can honeymoon or romance you and be on their best behavior for a short period of time. It is important for you not to believe that the honeymoon is a real indicator of change. The honeymoon is designed to get your guard down and to believe in them again so that they can continue to maintain the old controls. It is important to be skeptical of any sudden changes where they are pleasant and cooperative. An Avoider in recovery knows that playing on one's emotions can be hurtful to the person involved, and they will choose to keep exposing the ugliness of what they have done rather than want things to be radically changed for the good. You will need to use time as your indicator. If you settle for a honeymoon, it will only be a matter of time before the old avoiding behavior comes back and abuses you again. Hope is never sufficient impetus to change another person. Hope can cause you prematurely to encourage the Avoider when they are not in a place of change, and you will end up encouraging a honeymoon or a great stage performance, rather than real and lasting change. Reality is often painful to explore deeply, but it also permits change to happen. The old patterns will continue for years and even from generation to generation, if you are not willing to allow yourself to walk through the pain of reality and fight for lasting change.

Letting go of Quick Fixes

You need also to allow yourself not to emotionally reengage too quickly. The Avoider knows when he or she has you in the emotional place where he or she wants you to be. Avoiders want you to trust them and find them essential to meet your emotional *when we I started to relax & trust & enjoy her again she did the same thing she promised for she would never do again.*

Talking to Family Members

needs. They also want you to desire and long for things to be "normal" again. When an Avoider sees that you are back into the old comfort zones, he or she will know enough romancing has been done and now he or she can go back to getting personal needs met. Avoiders will not return to romance, unless you get fed up. As long as the family chooses to settle for a little romance, believing that something is better than nothing, the same old cycle will continue to repeat itself. ☆

Choosing Safe People

You need to stop believing that the Avoider will listen to your emotional pain. One of the big mistakes that a family makes with *me!* Avoiders is to keep wanting to share their feelings with the Avoider. Remember, if the Avoider truly heard your hurt and anger, he or she would show the fruit of repentance. If Avoiders are not showing the fruit of repentance, they will not be able to hear your hurt and anger appropriately. You need instead to stop believing that they are safe to share with. You need rather to begin to share your feelings of pain and anger to safe outside supports. To keep trying to share with the Avoider is to thwart your own quest for the support you deserve.

Secrecy is the prime weapon of Avoiders in marriage and other relationships. They want you to struggle alone and be convinced that you are a traitor if you talk to anyone else about the state of your marriage. Classic lines here are the following: "Our marriage is our life. You don't take personal stuff like this to others." "We need to be able to work this out between ourselves. If we can't work it out, how can we expect this marriage to survive?" "I would feel too ashamed if your family knew about this. Promise me that you will not embarrass me like that. I would never be able to look them in the eye again." You need to know that secrecy supports the problem because if it remains shrouded no one will confront the Avoider about it. You need to be willing to tell safe people how you are being affected by the Avoider. Tell people who are involved in both of your lives.

Quit trying to share anything w/ Dawn

The Trap of Enabling

It is vital that you choose not to be responsible for another's actions and you need to be able to separate yourself from being the problem. So many Indulgers in false guilt take on shame by association and such shame is dangerous to assume. Such shame extends false guilt to the extreme. The only legitimate guilt you should ever carry is if you chose to be an accomplice in the ongoing Avoider's sin. If you are currently choosing no longer to tolerate their sin, you do not need to blame yourself for "putting up with it for so long." You are doing now what is right. In confronting and no longer accepting what the Avoider is doing, you are actually choosing honesty and are yourself becoming clean. You are no longer any part of the problem and need to stop identifying yourself as such. Important steps for you to do to separate from the Avoider is to hope (but not falsely hope) that the Avoider may change, to work on choosing to see yourself as precious and worthy of being cherished, to set and keep loving limits for the Avoider, to continue to fight feeling any responsibility for choices outside of your own personal control, and to get the support you need that affirms that you are not at fault for the problem. You will be taking healthy steps of responsibility for yourself as you do these actions. The Avoider will likely be deeply threatened that you chose to take responsibility for yourself and to expose the shared problem. Realize that they feel threatened because they are feeding into their need for destructive control and this sickness and sin is causing them to feel threatened. You will likely be accused of betraying the relationship and your vow to God. You need to choose to be a "traitor" to the Avoider's sin pattern, or you will end up being an actual accomplice to their sin.

A helpful comparison is seen in the beloved child who is grown and is stealing from stores for drugs. Would you truly be caring for them if you encouraged their continued stealing and drug use? A caring parent chooses not to support their child in these self-destructive behaviors. Instead you choose to allow your child to face the consequences of his or her choices and hope and pray that the child will allow the consequences to change him or her.

Enabling the Indulger is also dangerous. Indulgers can consume tremendous amounts of emotional energy from those around them. At first glance this idea may seem odd. How can a person who appears invested primarily in doing for others consume emotional energy from them at the same time? Enabling the Indulger involves trying to convince them they are doing enough to be worthwhile. We discussed earlier how the Indulger is a "black hole" for reassurance. They never feel filled up, no matter how much encouragement is offered by friends and family. The antidote to enabling the Indulger is found in reinforcing the fact that God's grace is sufficient. When you feel pressured to reassure, direct the Indulger to go to neutral thinking, and later to focus on God's grace. Offering repeated reassurance may help the Indulger to feel better for the moment, but it ultimately helps them only to continue in their comfort zone.

Confronting the Avoider

You need also to become more willing to confront the Avoider by saying things like the following: "You're blaming me, and I won't take responsibility for what you are solely responsible for." "That was really controlling when you tried to entice me into pitying you. You tried to sidetrack me into not holding you responsible for what you've done. I care too much about you to let you get away with that control." "It's your choice to take responsibility or not, but if you don't take responsibility, I will not help or support you, and I would feel sad about the choices you made." "You are manipulating me with your anger right now, so I'm not willing to listen to you." "I'm sad that you see me as unloving, but I will continue not to allow you to manipulate me." "I know you see me as your judge, I cannot help that or change that, but it still does not change the fact that if you do _____ I will do _____ as a consequence of the choices you alone have made." "I'm very angry with you for trying to manipulate me. I will expose what you are doing to others if you continue." "You need to find healthy ways to get your needs met. Manipulating me is not one of those ways." "I'm interrupting you because not to interrupt you is to allow you to manipulate me and I will not let that happen anymore. I cannot help it if you see that as rude." "I know you want to focus on me right now, but that will only encourage you to avoid what you need to face. You can either choose to focus on yourself and what you are doing, or I will end this discussion." "If you start to manipulate me, I will stop talking with you." "I will not argue with you. It is pointless and only shows me that you want to manipulate me. I'm sad you are choosing this, but I won't be a part of it."

Calm in the Midst of a Storm

Make sure to be calm and avoid intense feelings when you make these statements or the Avoider will lose what you are saying and tend to focus on you as being irrational, too emotional, or out of control, and he or she will ignore what you have said and view you as the problem. Avoiders are likely to do this anyway, but you are in a healthier position when you can stop allowing them emotionally to engage you in behavior that's destructive to yourself. Even if you were emotional, or did not share your message in the best way, do not overcompensate. Apologize for the presentation, but stay firm on the message and repeat the essential issue in a calm way. Let the Avoider know that you are serious about the limits you will establish. Always follow through with the consequences you set or the encounter will be pointless.

Detouring Around Dead Ends

Realize that several words and phrases that we can often obsess about lead us into a dead-end road. Many people spend too much time and energy trying to figure out the "Why's" of any problem. The difficulty with "Why's" is that you end up trying to figure out how *you* can fix and solve things so that they do not happen again. This futile pursuit only makes you responsible for the problem, rather than allowing you to recognize and deal with the pain and anger you feel about being powerless in the situation that hurt you. Concentrate instead on "what can I do now to express my feelings and not be trapped by the past."

You will need to continue to be skeptical of the Avoider. You need to realize that at any time an Avoider can return to control. If they are in the healing process they will be able to tell you how you were affected by them in a way that captures your woundedness. They will put healing first. They will want to be accountable. They will be specific rather than vague. And most importantly, the Avoider will be focused on you rather than on him- or herself. Continue to set limits whenever control returns.

Encouraging the Indulger

While confrontation is an essential element in the change process, it must be approached differently with the Avoider and Indulger. We have encouraged frankness and a straightforward approach which brings the Avoider to face responsibility for the consequences of his or her actions. The Indulger is already extra-responsible and will take this approach as another opportunity to be disparaging and self-critical. Confronting the Indulger is best accomplished through an encouraging style.

We directed family members to make a list of costs incurred living with an Indulger. It may be helpful to review the list with the Indulger, emphasizing mutual responsibility. Explain to the Indulger how it hurts you when he or she does not believe your valuing of him or her. Share that it hurts when they do not believe or trust your true care.

You Are Precious

The next aspect of encouraging the Indulger involves God's valuing us as individuals. Indulgers minimize or discount the significance of God's valuing them. It is easy to get caught up in trying to counter the Indulger's negative self-comments and pessimism by giving examples of what a great person he or she is. As caring family you may want the person to focus on his or her strengths. A paradox is operative here which unfortunately works against the Indulger. He or she will take the positives noted and build higher and higher expectations for performance which ultimately lead to disappointment, confirming to the Indulger that he or she is not worthwhile after all.

The Indulger needs strong repeated reminders of the infinite value and worth which we all have in God's eyes, despite our accomplishments and how we may feel about ourselves at the moment. Simple phrases such as: "God loves me no matter what." "His grace is sufficient" or "God don't make no junk!" can serve as firm reminders of God's character. The Indulger is redirected to focus on God rather than on the false negative assumptions.

Finally, we want to encourage the family to be aware of your limitations. You are not a failure if you have not been able to change the one you love. You do not have to hate yourself for what you do not know. Allow yourself to release your unnecessary burdens by accepting help from those who have been trained to aid you with the frustrating impacts of inaction. Seeking help for yourself and challenging others to want help can bring about the process of healing.

Chapter Nine

Perspectives for Professionals who Offer Healing

The Avoider and Indulger have difficulty seeking the kind of counseling best suited to meet their unique needs. In our experience Avoiders and Indulgers approach counseling in a manner similar to the way they respond to God. That is, they choose the experience best suited to meet the needs of the opposite type of person. Avoiders seek counseling that focuses on empathy and encouragement which in turn minimizes the need to focus on their personal responsibility. Indulgers see counseling as a confrontive and directive process which painfully highlights their shortcomings.

The goal of this chapter is to make counselors aware of how their approach to the counseling process may inadvertently feed directly into the distortions of the Avoider and Indulger. Counselors are cautioned against underestimating the power of distorted guilt in the lives of their clients. Readers will learn more about the counseling process, enabling them to find a more appropriate client/counselor fit. Potential clients will be empowered to move through the counseling process.

We often counsel clients who have been disappointed with the approach taken by previous counselors. Despite their disappointment, these individuals typically were unable to discuss this feeling with the counselor. Avoiders may complain that the counselor was not sensitive or encouraging enough. Indulgers may suggest that the counselor seemed to listen a lot without really giving advice or direction about what to do next.

Dangers of Professional Codependency and Enabling

We have also seen counselors approach a variety of client needs and issues with an identical set of techniques and recommendations. This "one size fits all" approach to counseling flies in the face of a basic premise in this book: God speaks differently to different individuals because we tend to hear His message from different perspectives. Counselors who fail to be sensitive to client diversity risk being abusive to Indulgers and enabling the irresponsibility common in Avoiders.

We have observed that counselors more easily fall into the trap of enabling irresponsibility than of being demanding and abusive. Nevertheless, being demanding of Indulgers does take place.

Codependency on the part of the counselor involves the need to see others grow healthier to build the counselor's confidence or self esteem. This "need to fix others" impedes the counselor's ability genuinely to listen and be sensitive to the clients' issues. Indulgers believe that they are not worth being listened to. They feel like a burden and a drain on others. They do not have a realistic picture of their value and cannot believe that other people want to listen to and care for them. When counselors see their role as "fixing things," Indulgers get the message that they cannot do anything on their own. Do not give solutions, answers, or directions unless the Indulger already has a sense of personal value. Indulgers most need a listening and caring ear. Counselors encourage client codependency when they give solutions, rather than giving the message that they believe in and care about them. Instead, encourage them with words like, "I can listen and care, and I'd love to do that for you, because you matter to me." "I believe in you. I know what you need most is to have someone listen and care. I'd love to do that for you." Simply being an attentive and caring voice that longs to listen and love will do wonders and help bring about the healing in the Indulger's life.

Avoiders want answers too. They do not take responsibility for remembering the answers, but it makes them dependent on the counselor and able to blame you if things go wrong. This process fosters irresponsibility. The counselor who enables typically is ineffective in helping the Avoider change. Enabling encourages irresponsibility and avoiding his or her control issues. Counselors who enable are most often unable effectively to confront the Avoider with the reality of his or her destructive patterns. After discussing how to support the Indulger without fostering codependency we discuss how to confront the Avoider.

Supporting the Indulger

One of the best ways to support an Indulger is by developing good listening skills. Indulgers predict that no one will care enough to listen to them because they believe they are not valuable or worth enough to be listened to and loved. As they begin to tolerate being comforted they begin to grow and change.

Indulgers may need prompts to help them talk about their pain and anger. They have often been shamed in terrible ways. Maybe a therapist told them that their problem was that they expected too much and just could not forgive. Maybe important people have called them martyrs or told them that they complain too much. Indulgers will be overly sensitive to hearing those messages and will immediately shut down and feel shamed. Do not critique what they are saying. Do not point out victim thinking initially. Choose rather to reflect back the pain and anger that they feel and support what is healthy rather than focusing immediately in on the unhealthy. Applaud the courage it took for them to share with you. Tell them that it takes more courage to be vulnerable than to be all put together. Tell them you are glad they confided in you and that you hope they don't choose to avoid you by fearing that they have somehow burdened you. Reassure them that you care and want to be there for them now and also in the future.

Indulgers need encouragement to face painful emotions. The counselor can make short comments that support feelings. "It's okay to feel _____ (angry, hurt, scared, devastated, etc.)" "I'm here. I care. "I'm listening." "Let it out." "How incredibly _____ (painful, terrifying, horrible, etc.)." "I'm so sad you were hurt so badly." "You have every right to feel _____ (angry, hurt, etc.)." Validate the legitimacy of their feelings and encourage them to share their pain and anger with you, if they feel safe to do so.

Resist focusing on details, but instead look for the emotional content. Facts are never the critical area, but how one feels about the situation is essential to catch if you want to be a good listener. Be careful not to give answers or fix the situation. Answers often serve as a way the Indulger in false guilt will convict him- or herself further. He or she is unfamiliar with people who care enough just to listen to him or her. Just simply to be an attentive and caring voice that affirms and loves the Indulger will be significant and powerful.

Realize that clients fear silence when they are confiding. Indulgers in particular interpret silence to mean that people do not care about them, are bored, think they are wimpy and whining, are judging them or think that they are crazy. You want to voice small encouraging things that do not break the train of thought to help avoid the dangerous trap of self-judgment. Most people after they confide in you feel very vulnerable and scared. Ask them if they would like to know how you feel toward them. People then know what you may be thinking and can reduce their irrational fears. Such affirmation helps them not to feel so exposed. Tell them that you care. Say that you are proud of them for sharing. Ask them how you can continue to support them. Ask them what they need after being so courageously vulnerable. Explain how privileged you feel that they would trust you with such a precious part of themselves. Let them know that you do not mind reassuring them that you care. Let them know that if they get scared and can't remember that you care, that you will tell them again the truth of what you feel toward them. Reassure them that you understand their fear. Relate how scared you've been when you've taken risks, but how helpful that risk proved to be.

The counselor needs to become able to deal with intense emotions in the Indulger's experience.

Like one who takes away a garment on a cold day, or like vinegar poured on soda, is one who sings songs to a heavy heart. (Proverbs 25:20)

Indulgers will need the counselor to be able to deal with listening to intense anger and who will allow them to sob as a response to the agony in their souls. The counselor will need to choose to stay connected to their pain and anger. Anger is not wrong or bad, and nothing bad will happen because the client is angry. Listening is a powerful way to help the client to grow and to change for the better. Remember to stay away from feeling that you can change them or that the pain or anger will go away quickly. Recognize listening as a time investment in care for another. Avoid areas such as humor when someone has intense feelings. Avoid changing the subject or asking questions. Be very careful to stay engaged. The counselor needs to listen in a way that will allow you to reflect back what you heard them say. If the problem is the counselor's own discomfort or unease with the intensity of the emotions, share that with the Indulger. You as the counselor need to make it clear that it is your issue and not the Indulger's.

No Clichés Allowed

When listening, the counselor needs to be very careful to avoid giving "pat answers." For Christians, pat answers are made to sound spiritual, but rather are incredibly insensitive and inappropriate. They do not heal, they wound. They can cause Indulgers to mistrust faith and the church and not recognize the presence of God at a time of need. Typical pat answers for people in trauma are statements like the following: "God works all things for good," "forgive and forget," "leave the past behind you," "pray continuously," "give thanks in all circumstances," "trust God," etc. These pat phrases do not encourage Indulgers to grieve and experience the love of God through human vessels. Do not choose to exhibit behaviors that take Indulgers out of their feelings. The counselor needs to explore his or her own life and why you would insensitively give pat answers. Choose to help the person who is feeling by listening and caring. Remember, that someone who honestly wants to grieve and let go will know when they no longer need to feel strong emotions over particular situations. Clients will naturally let go and forgive when they have communicated their feelings enough.

Feelings in Their Proper Sphere

Be careful not to take responsibility for another person's involvement in processing their own emotions. The counselor must not feel the feelings for the person, but should allow his or her heart to empathize with clients as they experience relevant joy, sorrow and anger. If you are feeling overwhelmed by their pain, you are doing too much work that is rightfully the client's. Never feel more for another person than they are feeling for themselves or you will be taking on their work for them. Choose only to connect with the pain and anger they are sharing, even if their feelings are directed toward you.

The counselor needs to rehearse self-admonition such as, "choose to listen, they need me to hear them." "Even if they are angry, anger can help me understand them more and to grow myself." "I'm not responsible for fixing this situation, but rather to listen and to care." "Listening and caring are incredibly significant and are exactly what they need." Realize that good listening takes time and practice. Keep working to develop better skills. If you as the counselor did not listen the way you wish you would have, apologize, go back and try again.

Do not fear silence. Allowing for silence can give a wonderful message that I will wait for you to share the hard feelings on your heart. Silence gives a message of patience and kindness. It states that the client may take whatever time they need in the process of self-examination. Choose not to fill silences with idle words or with questions. Instead choose to say things like, "Take whatever time you need, I'm here and I care." The counselor needs to choose to allow him or herself to be comfortable with silence for the benefit of the client, while recognizing how the Indulger may misinterpret silence.

Be careful to avoid interrupting the person as he or she speaks. An Indulger in false guilt has a strong belief (though not true, it is very powerful) that no one will want to listen to him or her. If you as the counselor cut the Indulger off, he or she is likely to shut down altogether and see your interruption as a statement that you really did not want to hear him or her. Indulgers look for any signs to justify or prove their sense of being unworthy. Strive to avoid the potential traps these individuals can use to support their distorted belief.

Creative Reassurance

Remind them that sharing their pain once will not be enough although they initially may think so. They will need to learn to tolerate painful self-examination coupled with ongoing love and support. Encourage them by saying that you would eagerly continue to listen to them and that you realize that they will need to talk and talk and talk about their grief. Choose to give them statements that specifically allow them to realize that you want to be there because you care about them as individuals.

When they seem to be avoiding their emotions by asking for solutions and answers to their problems, let them know that you feel uncomfortable giving them solutions when such shortcuts only allow them to avoid their deeper feelings. Reassure them that you believe the most important thing for them to do is to become aware of their painful feelings and that they will be able to make healthier decisions when they have processed their emotions well. Let them know that you believe in them and believe that they themselves are able to discover the answers that fit who they are and where they are in their lives. Share your concerns over choices they are making that do not support their deep intrinsic value, but do not make decisions for them. Be careful to not foster an unhealthy dependence on you. Such dependence allows them to give you responsibility for emotional work that they should be doing for themselves, rather than encouraging responsibility for and ownership of their own personal choices. Remember that your best support for them is shown as you listen, share your concerns, and care.

Realize that Indulgers will feel that they are betraying others when they express their own feelings about them. They will feel that they are misrepresenting the other person and making you see these others in a highly unflattering light. They will believe that you will perceive the other person as a terrible, horrible monster, and they will back away from portraying anyone in a way that could be misunderstood. Reassure Indulgers that you do not see them as the source of these difficulties. Encourage them with the truth that it is good for them to expose their pain and anger. Let them know that you do not see them as betraying anyone. Reassure them that you are not rigid in your thinking and will not see only the negatives in the other person. Remind them that sincere love hates what is evil, but holds fast to what is good (Romans 12:9). The counselor needs to give Indulgers the message that you are glad that they talked. Share your concern that their fears keep them from trusting themselves. The counselor needs to encourage them to step away from assuming they are the source of the problem, and encourage them rather to detach from taking responsibility for another person's choices.

Helpful Strategies for Indulgers

There are some exceptions to the listening rules. If you have good reasons to believe the client is lying, do not support lies, as they will only hurt your client in the end. Other people who should not be encouraged to grieve are people who have borderline personality disorder or histrionic personality disorder. These people indulge in extremes with their feelings and become easily overwhelmed and hopeless, with such feelings even leading them to consider suicide. First establish emotional groundedness and balance with feelings, for only then will the processing of emotions be fruitful. They need to establish healthy boundaries with their emotions or chaos will ensue.

"A Woman's Prerogative" (and a Man's!)

Remind Indulgers that they can always do "after the fact" work which means that they can change their minds. Most Indulgers believe if they made a promise, even if the promise was unhelpful or sabotaging to themselves, they have to follow through with whatever they promised. Remind them that they can always backpedal, state why they changed their mind, and do what they wish they would have done initially. Encourage them to go back and redo the situation as soon as they realize the problem, and do what they wish they would have done originally. Help them to see that they can apologize for their error, but then do not need to follow through with the unhealthy promise.

Challenge them to see that repentance is critical for their loved ones. Help them to sort out whether it is a "sorrow that leads to death" or if it is a "sorrow that leads to life." Challenge them to look for the specific fruit of repentance in those around them. Encourage them to hold out for sincere repentance. Remind them that God has given them fruit to look for that will allow them to assess where the loved one is on the journey toward repentance. God wants both you as counselor and the Indulger client to make these kinds of determinations.

Truth Will Set Them Free

Push the Indulger to choose to see reality even when that reality is agonizing. Lacking recognition does not make problems go away. Encourage him or her that you will walk with him or her and hold him or her accountable to move toward lasting changes. Let Indulgers know that if they need someone to go with them to confront the other person that you would be willing to encourage them and help them identify those who would be helpful supports. Let them know that if they need to talk before or after a confrontation you will be willing to listen to them.

Boundaries

Remember that Indulgers have incredible difficulty setting limits. They often go backward rather than forward, and will need much reassurance, patience, and reality testing to help them set the limits they need and to keep them focused away from taking responsibility for the other person's issues.

Encourage Indulgers to trust their gut. Perceptions of reality become highly inaccurate as soon as Indulgers question their intuition. They need to be encouraged to trust their initial reaction in a give situation. Again an exception should be made if there is evidence they are believing lies.

Encourage them to read books like this one or books on codependency or family of origin. Pretending will never make any problem go away. Encourage them to attend support groups like Codependency Anonymous, Al-Anon, or other "Anon" groups, ACOA, sexual abuse support groups, or any emotional processing support group. Challenge them to go to the groups and talk about themselves. Challenge them to focus in on themselves rather than on the other people in the group. Encourage them to get out and participate in activities they enjoy and to care for themselves by treating themselves like God's precious children.

It is important that the counselor never tell a client that he or she has a problem the person does not see. This is suggestion, and clients are vulnerable to suggestion. When clients describe what they see as fact, reflect the fact back and let the client decide what that means. Resist pressuring the client to accept your interpretation of a given situation which could foster the use of your position as a counselor to simply control others. Assure them they can change their opinion if later they gather new information. Much balance and no control are needed in this area, so clients can be empowered to make their own choices. It is wrong for the counselor to push his or her agenda on a client. Such manipulation hurts the client and it does not recognize that God will empower the client to make decisions about his or her life.

Confronting the Avoider

You as counselor will need to give yourself much mental reaffirmation as you detach from taking responsibility from Avoiders of true guilt. A natural place to struggle is to feel that you are being cruel and unfair to the client. Perhaps you feel that you have not given them enough chances and are being irrationally demanding. These distortions keep the counselor an accomplice to the Avoider's offenses against God and others. The counselor's perceived cruelty needs to be reframed as lovingly refusing to assume an obligation for others' responsibilities. The client may respond as would a child in a tantrum. They often express disdain for the counselor, just as would the overwrought child, but your actions are loving and are helping the child or adult to mature in healthy ways if they go on to choose healthy patterns. The counselor's responsibility is to provide significant consequences for the out-of-control child or adult and to stay firm and not give in when the pressure rises and it becomes difficult no longer to support old unhealthy behaviors.

Stay focused on spiritual truths. The manipulator or Avoider takes concepts of scripture and distorts them as a way to manipulate situations to his or her own satisfaction. Let's explore some Biblical truths that you can to begin to ground yourself in.

More Than Just, "I'm Sorry"

Biblically, forgiveness has never been, and will never be simply saying "I'm sorry." We explored the fullness of this concept in Chapter Six, when we discussed how the Avoider can choose personal change. The Bible demands repentance. Repentance can specifically identify the wrong done to another; it displays an indignation for the wrong; it longs for restored relationships; it desires to make amends to clear the situation; and it desires to face whatever consequences or punishments are needed to restore the relationship or to help the wounded to feel safe (2 Corinthians 7:8-13).

The most loving and compassionate things we can ever do for people are to hold them responsible for themselves and their actions and to hope and pray that they make good choices. Enablers are skilled at clinging to what is good and working to redefine evil as good. God states that sincere love does not make evil look good. Instead sincere love hates that which is evil and harmful to others. Would you truly love your precious child if someone injured them wrongly and you did not fully embrace and hate the wrong done to them? Likewise, you need to choose to hate the wrong done to others. This is what scripture calls sincere love. Enabling and calling evil acceptable is not love.

> In a large house there are articles not only of gold and silver, but also of wood and clay; some are for noble purposes and some for ignoble. If a man cleanses himself from the latter, he will be an instrument for noble purposes, made holy, useful to the Master and prepared to do any good work. Flee from evil desires of youth, and pursue righteousness, faith, love and peace, along with those who call on the Lord out of a pure heart. Don't have anything to do with foolish and stupid arguments, because you know that they produce quarrels. And the Lord's servant must not quarrel; instead, he must be kind to everyone, able to teach, not resentful. Those who oppose him he must gently instruct, in the hope that God will grant them repentance leading them to a knowledge of the truth, and that they will come to their senses and escape from the trap of the devil, who has taken them captive to do his will. (2 Timothy 2:20-26)

This passage emphasizes the counselor's need to step away from feeling that he or she is a participant in the situations others may want us to be a part of. We are also challenged no longer to share in the evil behaviors of the Avoider. It is important to begin to separate ourselves from the equation of evil and to see the

Avoider as the participant in the ignoble, and to allow ourselves to be a participant in the noble. God states that He can use us then, and He will prepare us to do good work. We need to work to keep our hearts pure, and to choose love and peace to separate ourselves from the ignoble. We need to disengage from foolish, fruitless arguments designed to manipulate us and to enable the Avoider. We must really begin to understand that the more we participate in a quarrel, the more we are really only fueling the Avoider's belief that he or she can manipulate us. Arguments keep us from confronting real issues and allow us to get sidetracked from holding the Avoiders responsible for their issues. Begin to say things such as, "I'm not going to argue with you. You can choose to manipulate, but I can choose to have consequences for that manipulation. I'd be sad if you make poor choices, but I need to let you do it. I will not argue with you, though." The scripture passage encourages you to be gentle yet firm and include appropriate responses for the inappropriate choices.

The Avoider will try to convince the counselor that dredging up the past does not help forgiveness. Scripture never tells us to leave the past in the past if this leaving is a way to cover up sin and no longer to fight against evil. Remember that scripture defines sincere love as hating what is evil and holding fast to what is good. 1 Peter 2:16 states, "Live as free men, but do not use your freedom as a cover-up for evil; live as servants of God." This passage emphasizes that grace was never designed to help people avoid their sin. Grace always fully exposes sin. If we turn from the sin and allow God to control our lives, He will give us the freedom He longs for us to have. Do not ignore unrepentant sin from Avoiders or permit currently destructive patterns they are still embracing. Such conduct will only enable the patterns to continue and keep the Avoider from needing to move toward repentance. It will also continue to foster the distorted thinking which is so prevalent in the Avoider of true guilt. Avoiders need to choose always to be aware of their sin. Being aware of sin does not keep one a slave to it. Rather, such awareness can empower one to avoid and flee from the areas that are problematic for him or her, so that one will continue to move in the direction of emotional health and freedom. Scripture in the Old Testament commands the Israelites to remember what happened in the wilderness, so that this recollection should keep them from going back into their former sin patterns. God left them in the wilderness for forty years because they had no desire to change or to repent. God does not force change, but He will not allow the unrepentant to enter the promised land and neither should we as counselors. Do not reward someone's distorted thinking and lack of repentance. The counselor will always need to choose to confront sin patterns in order to foster client growth in the healing process.

Faithful Are the Wounds of a Friend

Antiseptic for Avoiders of true guilt, at best, is sure to make them angry with you, and at worst, will lead them to leave the counseling relationship. Initially in some way you will appear to them to be their enemy unless they are incredibly good at people-pleasing and then you will be their silent enemy. The Avoider's defenses will likely increase. To be a antiseptic giver, you must choose to know and memorize the games the Avoider is likely to play so you are not thrown by them and you are no longer surprised by his or her manipulative strategies. You want to arrive at a place where the Avoider's typical defenses become highly predictable to you, as we hope the counseling strategies will also become familiar to you.

A helpful way to clarify your counseling strategies is by looking at the situation as if the Avoider were a rebellious child who had been given many chances for repentance and at grace, but was still participating in sin and rebellion. You would realize that letting the child continue willful misbehavior without consequences was unproductive and our hope is that you would see the need to allow adverse results for this behavior. These principles are not just for children. Work has consequences. If you show up drunk, you would be sent home or possibly fired. If you fail to show up at work, you can be given a written reprimand, and if you fail to be sufficiently cooperative in the daily workload you will lose your job. These are not just principles for the young, but are principles designed to hold people responsible for their own choices throughout life. No one forces the man to show up late and forfeit his employment. Forfeit simply results where significant warning of the impending consequences of poor choices was given, and those choices persisted.

The Father Disciplines for Our Good

A quality important in antiseptic-givers is the willingness to set consequences for poor choices and not to be persuaded that you are being a dictator, are treating the Avoider like a child, or are controlling. As on the job, you are simply asking him or her to be a team player on a team they chose to join. They need to play by the rules for the health of the team or the team will lose and become ineffective. You as an antiseptic-giver provide clients the choice to get extra training so they can be effective, or to lose their position on the team. The choice is theirs. It is not your choice.

The Power of Choice

To hold Avoiders responsible for their choices rather than to accept personal responsibility from them is critical to the recovery process. Counselors assume too much responsibility when they feel that they are the cause of the Avoider's defenses, and that if the counselor simply made things more clear to the Avoider, the Avoider would be able and willing to change. You cannot make them change, you can only clarify the consequences for lack of change and choose to follow through with these consequences. A good captain takes those duties very responsibly. Some captains are captains by default. The natural leader has stepped aside and is no longer coaching. You can choose to have no coach, or to step in and coach. God has designed men to lead the household, not authoritatively, but in love. When the male steps down from that leadership, the female must choose to take the captain position by default, and challenge the old captain to relearn the skills he needs to be effective again. You as the counselor can encourage individuals to be healthy even if their spouses choose unhealthy ways.

Game rules for a winning season include the counselor persevering in detaching from responsibility for others. A coach does not take responsibility for members of his team outside of describing to them their needed duties and applying consequences when they fail to complete their tasks. You as a counselor-coach are responsible for caring for yourself, and for telling the team what you believe they need to accomplish to operate successfully. If you are investing your energies in the impossible task of changing others, you are failing to invest that energy in yourself. You are the only person God will hold you responsible for changing. The object of these practical steps for change is not to change Avoiders. It is rather to respect and honor yourself enough that you do not allow yourself to be manipulated and deceived by behavior that leads only continued sin. You will also choose to stop being an accomplice to sin by detaching from taking responsibility for another's actions.

Misusing Antiseptic

Not all counselors have the temperament or training effectively to confront clients who need emotional cleansing. Scripture states we need not to provide antiseptic if it is a way to repay evil for evil (1 Thessalonians 5:14-15), for we need to do it with kindness. We need to do it for God and to give Him the praise for any positive outcomes (Colossians 3:15-16). Confronting with gentleness and kindness involves maintaining a heartfelt desire for another's good, and a longing for the person to "repent and live." If you do not truly want another person to grow, change and heal, do not be an antiseptic-giver. If you hate another person and your words are an attack, do not offer antiseptic. If you are saying what you are saying because you are tired of the person or are simply exhausted, say nothing. If you are confronting as a way for an emotional vent for yourself, say nothing. If your heart does not want them to change, say nothing. If you want them to change for your benefit rather than for their own benefit, say nothing. If fixing others is a way for you to escape from yourself, say nothing. Emotional cleansing is effective only when it serves to meet Christ's second command of "Love your neighbor as yourself."

Confronting wrong life patterns has pitfalls. You must be willing to be hated if you are going to disinfect a toxic lifestyle. Clients initially may not understand your compassion or care, and they will, very sincerely at that time, see you only as the enemy. You must prepare yourself for such an attack just as the mother would before she applies antiseptic to her child's wounds. She is sorry that the child needs it, but she does not allow her sympathetic feelings to divert her from doing what is right and loving toward her child. You will need to reassure yourself often that what you are doing is compassionate and right, even though the results of the healing are not immediate. The confrontive therapist is appreciated only when clients realize that without the treatment and confrontation, no healing would occur. Unfortunately, for counselors there is often a huge gap of time between the beginning of intense disdain and the recognition of healing. Understanding occurs when healing begins.

So how do you as a counselor choose to be a cathartic healer? This learned task may breed much initial tension and fear. You will need single-mindedly to concentrate on the picture of your client as a hurting, precious child who would be far worse off without your medication. Much mental reassurance will remind you of how loving it is to provide antiseptic. You learn phrases such as, "I know you hate me now. I hope someday you will see how difficult it is for me to care for you in this confrontive way. I will always want your complete healing, no matter what choices you make." Or "Your healing is so important to me that I am willing to risk your hating me and maybe never understanding that I cared tremendously."

Helpful to the counselor is the reminder that doing the same thing the same way will never bring behavioral change. Rather, remind yourself to refuse to encourage the same old behaviors in your clients and you will offer them hope and potential for change. Also remind yourself of the damage you can do when you enable, and that only "enemies multiply kisses." You will need strong prayer support behind you. Pray for the ability to care and for the revelation of God's truth through the scriptures. Ask for accountability from safe people in your own efforts not to enable. Utilize a healthy support network of other care givers who will hold you responsible for your own health as a counselor.

1 Peter 3:13-18 addresses another way to stay grounded when beginning the journey of changing the way you relate to others:

> Who is going to harm you if you are eager to do good? But even if you should suffer for what is right, you are blessed. "Do not fear what they fear; do not be frightened." But in your hearts set apart Christ as Lord. Always be prepared to give an answer to everyone who asks you to give the reason for the hope that you have. But do this with gentleness and respect, keeping a clear conscience, so that those who speak maliciously against your good behavior in Christ may be ashamed of their slander. It is better, if it is God's will, to suffer for doing good than for doing evil. For Christ died for sins once for all, the righteous for the unrighteous, to bring you to God.

We are reminded of what Christ did for us, as He challenges us to have a heart of compassion even for those who revile you for urging their change. This passage does not state that God wants you to martyr yourself. God challenges us to love even when people hate us for it. He will see and know what you are doing and honor you for it. This is not a license to stay in an abusive situation. God clearly calls us to confront and set limits. Again this passage is designed to help us fight for lovingly-set limits even when people despise us for keeping these boundaries. We must be careful, as Christ would, to strike the loving balances that allow us to live by scriptures rather than to misuse them.

Letting Go

When I (Karen) I began doing therapy I struggled with believing that it was right for me to work harder than others were working for their own recovery. Let me give you some background. When I was in graduate school, I worked as a psychological technician on a hospital wing. A person with whom I had spent time was deeply suicidal. I tried to warn everyone I could that he was not safe and would kill himself. A co-worker of mine several weeks after he was discharged brought in his obituary to me saying, "Wasn't this your friend, Karen?" He had killed himself, just as I was sure he would.

My heart grieved. I know what it is like to have someone I cared about die and be powerless to prevent it. I thought I had reconciled to this, but when I started being responsible for clients I worked with after finishing school, I found myself doing what I now know to be an insanity pattern. I seemed subconsciously to feel that I should have been able to do something to save my friend, and I carried this on into my new work as a professional psychotherapist. My first career job was also in a hospital so I had plenty of opportunity to be with truly suicidal people. I worked diligently to keep one woman alive and nothing changed in her life. She would have a "yes but..." for everything I suggested. I was very frustrated that I wasn't giving her the hope she needed to make her want to live, so I tried even harder. Unfortunately, those efforts didn't make her want to live either.

I started having numerous physical symptoms arising from my own terrible anxiety about not being able to save her. A co-worker friend of mine saw my frenzy and gently told me, "Karen, you need to let go and let her die." I couldn't believe his words. I was very angry with him and believed that he just did not care enough or just did not truly understand the situation. I tried harder still, but I was still not attaining the goal I wanted. I went back to my co-worker out of desperation to get some new ways to try harder, only to get those same terrible words again, "Karen, you are working harder for her than she is for herself. That will never help her or you. You must let her go even if that means she dies." I struggled with this, but the next day, with tears in my eyes, I told the woman that I needed to let her die, because she did not want to live and saw no hope in her situation, and I was not powerful enough to make her live. She was shocked. She said, "You're going to let me die?" I remember saying through God's help, "I have no other choice. You don't want to live, and I don't have the power to keep you alive against your will." She said, "So you think there is no hope?" I said, "You have never chosen to hold onto hope, so I realize that you will probably end up dead, and I need to stop holding on and let you make your own choice even if, my friend, that would mean I need to grieve your loss." Miraculously, as often results from surrender, she did not choose death, but my relinquishment helped her fight for her life herself, because I was no longer doing her work for her. I could never have predicted that outcome. I was prepared to have her die.

A word of caution here is that the concept of surrender should never be used as a manipulative tool in an attempt to make God give us the outcome we want. For example, if I now say, "Hey it works to tell someone suicidal that I need to let them die. I can keep them alive when I do that." I believe if I did that now, I would be manipulating God and playing Russian Roulette with my client. Surrender is being willing to believe that God has the outcome in His hands no matter what. You have no idea what will happen, and you must not be focused on the outcome, but rather on obedience to Christ and His kingdom. Letting go does not mandate a happy outcome. I believe if God's outcome was death, I would have a trial of grief and guilt to work through that God could use to produce positive results in my life. I believe I would come face to face with the ugliness of sin and the foolish illusion of man's control. I believe surrender is the only choice to make.

God is able to work in our lives when we surrender our need to control the outcomes. These concepts have become incredibly real to me. I realize that I did not keep that woman alive; it was an utterly miraculous act of God for which I am deeply grateful. Letting go is hard initially. It seems such a foolish thing to do, as dangerous as walking out into a busy street blindfolded. Your death is imminent and only a fool would let go. That's what surrender feels like, but a loving, powerful God stands in control of all results and longs for us to experience peace and surrender.

Christ's Touch Changes Us

Chapter Ten

The Church and the Healing Process

Throughout the New Testament, the church is described as a place where believers can find support on their spiritual journeys. The church today continues to be a widely underutilized resource in the healing process, for individuals often hesitate to make use of the church because of negative past experiences. Unfortunately, congregations, pastors, and leaders have at times failed to meet the needs of some individuals, and in some cases have actually contributed to the problems people experience in life. Perhaps those in need have no idea what to expect and let fear keep them from seeking pastoral help. We want to encourage people to look for the help the church has to offer. This chapter provides an overview of issues germane to Avoiders and Indulgers and their relationship to the church. The goal of this discussion is to provide direction for church leaders and members, to help them to avoid perpetuating the development of Avoiders and Indulgers within their congregations, first by emphasizing the positive aspects of guilt. Second, the church body needs to strive to balance confrontation and support. Soft-pedaling the truth promotes avoiding guilt, while legalism promotes indulging in false guilt.

We recognize the difficult place the church is in. Church leadership often has minimal ongoing contact with people who are hurting, but is often expected by a family to provide a rapid cure for any problem. Because God has given a special authority to the church, it is vital for the church to be actively involved in the healing process.

Part of the Solution and Part of the Problem

The church provides a tremendous community of individuals who can serve one another by supporting efforts to better cope with life's difficulties. Throughout the New Testament the apostle Paul recounts his many fond memories of the positive support he had received in the various churches he visited. He exhorted these churches to keep providing similar support to others. We can look to these accounts of the early church as positive and uplifting examples of what the church may provide. Today's church offers a wide variety of support, including Bible studies to provide fundamental truths, share groups for loving support, and prayer meetings for taking people's hurts seriously. Many churches even offer benevolence funds to help pay for counseling in the event the church is unable to meet the need. Some churches also provide trained counselors as part of their ministry.

It is often easy to take pot shots at the church. People expect to find perfection and health in the body of the church, failing to realize that the church is actually made up of individuals, each striving to find his or her way along a personal spiritual journey in relationship with Christ. These unrealistic expectations lead to disappointment and disillusionment with what the church is and what it offers in the way of healing. It is ironic that people need the church to be full of healthy individuals while Christ's message was that He came to minister to the sick (Matthew 9:12).

While the church can provide resources to meet a great number of needs, the church is not a universal provider of help. The church has limitations which can be fostered by difficulties with church leadership and lack of commonality in goals and purpose. These kinds of difficulties are not new. Paul confronted similar problems in the church at Philippi (Philippians 2:1-4). The solution to this sort of difficulty is to approach one another with the kind of humility demonstrated by Christ.

There is an old saying that provides some further insight about the difficulties found in the church, "Hurt people, hurt people." This saying suggests that we tend to damage others in relationships in large part because we have been damaged ourselves. Since the church is full of individuals who have been hurt in the past, there are bound to be ongoing difficulties with relationships among church attendees. We hope that you will be encouraged to see positive aspects of what the church offers and not allow perceived negatives to block access to needed support.

Another problem you will likely encounter if you choose to be a church that challenges grace in real life situations with real people is that you may quickly become overwhelmed by the many people within your church who are struggling with a misunderstanding of grace. It is then easy to lose hope that anything can be done. This is a good place to heed Jethro's advice to Moses which was to delegate responsibilities or you will burn out (Exodus 18:14-27). People who have experienced the freedom of God's grace are very humbled and grateful and are often excited to help those who struggle: to whom much is given, much is expected (Luke 12:48).

Finally, certain elements in the church work at cross purposes with God's methods of healing. We have established that God works differently with each of us, based on our needs and sensitivities to hearing His message. The church can provide needed information and instruction for developing keen sensitivity to God's redirection through guilt. Nevertheless, the church can fail to provide a balanced perspective on the issue of guilt, which in the end encourages the development of destructive patterns in both the Avoider and Indulger.

Soft-Pedaling the Truth

Avoiders tend to flourish in environments where personal responsibility is minimized. Some churches approach scripture with concern that individuals are turned away from God's messages when His truths are boldly put forth. While Indulgers in false guilt tend to struggle in response to this kind of approach, the Avoider is enabled to ignore God's call to repentance.

Another difficulty we see the church struggling to deal with is tough love. The church is in a precarious position to balance limit setting. No matter where the line is drawn, different individuals will see it as harsh, appropriate, or too liberal. We are excited to see churches working hard to follow God's direction in this area.

Paul addressed this issue with the Corinthian church. This church had been struggling with a man who was involved in immorality, but had continued to accept him as part of their meetings. This man was apparently not repenting of his actions, nor stopping them, even though he was continuing to be involved with the church. Paul directed the church to cease enabling this man to avoid the reality and consequences of his actions. Paul instructed them to stop associating with the man in order to help him see that his sin would cost his position in the church and his relationships with the other members. Paul suggests that this strategy would allow sin to come to full exposure before God and others. The end result of the church's action was that the man did see the errors of his way, he repented, and was brought back into the fellowship of the church.

Some congregations are unwilling to take a firm stance in response to sin and destructive behavior on the part of members. Still other churches have explicitly endorsed alternative life-style choices and other depravity by those in leadership positions. Such responses minimize the special role God has developed for the church, and cloud the sin issue for the individuals involved in avoiding such guilt. Extenuating sin by the church salves the conscience of the Avoider, and thus contributes to the ongoing development and support of the Avoider's destructive behavior choices.

Another hurtful imbalance to be cautioned against is placing too much emphasis on support. Support without confrontation simply enables sin as the Avoider escapes the consequences God may be trying to use to call him or her to repentance. The opposite perspective yields damaging results. Confrontation without support places an unbalanced importance on law over grace. This

The Church and the Healing Process

extreme overemphasizes harshness and criticism, promoting indulgence in false guilt.

Legalism and the Indulger

Indulgers in false guilt are encouraged to develop destructive patterns when legalism and confrontation are emphasized above God's grace. Remember that the Indulger is hypersensitive to the issue of repentance, actively seeking to take responsibility for and to repent of things over which he or she has no legitimate control.

In his letter to the Roman church, Paul emphasized the critical importance of balancing law and grace. Paul realized that Indulgers needed redirection and encouragement to see God's grace. In 1 Corinthians 7:15-24, Paul stressed the importance of being free from indulging in false guilt when he exposed the slavery some were indulging in over the issue of circumcision. Paul indicated that overstressing this particular issue clouded the more important issue of growing in one's relationship with God.

Please do not choose to over-utilize the excessive responsibility of Indulgers. They have difficulty saying "No," and are easily swayed by any pressure or guilt. Please choose instead to find out if they are taking care of themselves. Encourage them to have time to focus and reflect on how valuable they are to God. Let them know that you will love them even if they are unable to participate in numerous church activities.

Some churches stress the importance of external appearances or an intricate set of specific behaviors that are required to be part of "the group." This perspective underemphasizes the special place we each have in relation to God: We are His precious creation whom He values beyond measure. Indulgers seem to be attracted to the types of church environments that promote such an emphasis on man's depravity. They are reminded over and over again of their shortcomings. Such reminding serves to reinforce the negative self-beliefs which perpetuate the Indulger's feelings of inadequacy. Indulgers in these environments work harder and harder to earn value in the sight of God, yielding great benefits for the church and church leadership, but at great psychological, physical and spiritual cost to themselves.

Balancing Confrontation and Support

Many times sermons are directed to one of the audiences in the congregation: either the Avoider or the Indulger. Unfortunately, if our premises are accurate, the Indulger hears confrontation and exhortation rather than empathy and God's valuing, and the Avoider hears valuing and empathy rather than confrontation and consequences. Avoiders feel loved in their active sin, and Indulgers feel condemned in light of their overactive consciences. Pastors must be aware of this dynamic so that you can warn of the potential ways people will misuse sermons to stay away from God's rich grace. When we teach our clinic programs we always give a warning to clients of ways they may misconstrue what is being taught, and thus be enabled to stay stuck rather than move toward God's grace. What we will typically say is "This concept is more addressed to Indulgers. It would be wise for those of you who know you need to look at how you have hurt others and are controlling, to avoid seeing yourself as a victim. Instead I hope you will understand that what is being taught can show you how people that you have hurt are affected." We cannot guarantee the message will not be distorted, but we do warn clients. This strategy can be helpful in the church context as well.

Successful ministry through the church provides confrontation and support reflecting aspects of God's law and God's grace. It is crucial for church leadership to emphasize the proper part of God's messages for the right audience. Leadership needs to confront sin and require responsible action in the Avoider. Failure to confront simply enables the Avoider to continue sinning. Confrontation drives the Indulger into deeper self-condemnation and shame. Failure to provide support and emphasize God's grace simply does not meet the needs of the Indulger. The church is in an extraordinary position to provide for the needs of both the

Avoider and Indulger through balancing confrontation and support.

Working Together

Many issues in life are not specifically addressed by Scripture. The Bible does however provide basic principles and direction in life. If you do not know how to help people move to spiritual truths through very practical suggestions, refer them to appropriate counselors. Pastors have often not been trained to deal with many areas people struggle with and thus can feel overwhelmed by them. An example of pathology needing professional counsel is obsessive compulsive disorder. Other examples are histrionic and borderline personality disorders. Many pastors are unaware of signs of psychosis, while others also have not learned how to deal with anxiety problems. We as counselors can be your resource suppliers. We can inform you about helpful directions in which to point troubled parishioners while not superseding your ultimate higher authority in the church. We recognize and respect your governing role and believe that we can provide vital insights to the body of the church, freeing you to do what you do best—minister God's love and grace.

Many counselors have failed to support pastors. They do not involve them in client treatment and they do not respect their unique position of authority in the church. We believe this is a grave mistake. The church is more important than a counseling clinic. We exist only as a supplement to help the church in its ministry to believers and seekers. Counselors need actively to involve and encourage church leadership to become part of the therapy process. We want to encourage you to ask your parishioner who goes into professional counseling to include you in the journey toward emotional healing. Call the therapist if he or she does not call you. Working together is a gift of love we can jointly give to the hurting person.

Let's cooperate with one another. We share a common goal. We hope you as the church will allow us as counselors to share the wisdom God has given each of us. We hope counselors will affirm to the church the authority God has given to it. We will be helping spread the real message of the gospel as we work together.

Chapter Eleven
Final Words to Encourage

Throughout this book we have described what we believe are central aspects of the emotional healing process. Healing God's way is not an easy process but is one with rich rewards for those who have the courage to pursue the journey. We hope you have been challenged and motivated to surrender your control to God, which is the first step in healing. The goal of healing is to bring repentance and growth in your relationship with God. A more intimate walk with God brings tremendous benefits in every area of life!

Closer with God
God longs to meet our heart's desires. His best for us is the only thing that will satisfy our soul thirst. Our hearts are unsettled until they are rejoined with their first love, God. God alone brings freedom, for His love covers a multitude of sins (James 5:20).

God has an incredible ability instantly to release a situation and forgive us for ways we have wronged Him.

> For as high as the heavens are above the earth, so great is his love for toward those who fear him; as far as the east is from the west, so far has he removed our transgressions from us. As a father has compassion on his children, so the Lord has compassion on those who fear him... (Psalm 103:11-13)

> I, even I, am he who blots out your transgressions for my own sake, and remembers your sins no more." (Isaiah 43:25)

I have swept away your offenses like a cloud, your sins like the morning mist. Return to me, for I have redeemed you." (Isaiah 44:22)

He will forgive only when there is true repentance, but it appears that He does not need to do any emotional work before He takes us back into His heart. As He draws us back, God's grace brings deep comfort for both the Avoider and Indulger.

While God's grace allows "fast track" renewal in our relationship with Him, we must continue to face the long-term consequences of scars left behind. The scars are much more difficult to heal in our relationships with other people. We as humans do not have that same ability to let go of significant wounds "in a flash." Healing in relationships is empowered as the repentant person listens to the wounded person recount the incredible pain and anger caused by the wound. This process begins to heal the repentant person, and it helps them stay in touch with the damage they caused, which is the best motivator to change old behaviors. This interaction helps the wounded to let go of the pain and to restore trust with the offender, if the offender sincerely repents and begins to listen and care about what they did. God encourages us over and over again in the Old Testament to remember and recount the ways the nation of Israel struggled in the wilderness. Celebrations were designed specifically for this task. God understood that, for us, it is important to not forget but to remember sin in order to embrace fully the awesomeness of God's grace and mercy, and to attain accountability for avoiding habitual sin patterns in the future. Remembering for a repentant person means being grateful to God for the miracle of forgiveness. Remembering may be used by the Indulger for self punishment, but it need not be used that way. Remembering is especially difficult for the Avoider, but is necessary to help cement change.

To Those With Hardened Hearts

We hope you have been touched by God's grace as you read this book. However, it is possible you have failed to identify with either the Avoider or Indulger. We believe there is a little of both in each of us. Developing sensitivity to God's calling is crucial. God may use stiff measures to provoke our repentance. Family and friends need to maintain firm limits not to tolerate your sin. If repentance has not occurred, our hope for you is that life will become harder and more confusing for you until you are forced to confront the God you are rebelling against. We hope someday you will embrace God's grace fully. We also hope someday to celebrate with you and embrace that change. For those who have experienced such change, the gratitude and rejoicing that result are among the earth's grandest celebrations to share.

Reconciliation

Forgiveness yields reconciliation as the final phase in the healing process. Our hope is that if you have been wounded by an Avoider of true guilt and they show the fruit of repentance, you would choose to participate in the process of reconciliation. Reconciliation occurs in a healthy way when you begin to take risks in whatever safe way you feel (some choose therapy sessions or having trusted friends present) as you begin to share your hurt and anger. You will expose the full damage of the wound done to you. A repentant person will listen and understand the healing power of hearing the reality of what they have done to you and to others. They will embrace the pain of this journey. God calls us to forgive the person regardless of their repentance or lack of it. The beauty of reconciliation is the special rejoining God has had with us through salvation, and that we are able to have with others who choose the path of repentance.

God calls us to forgive. He realizes that even if someone does not repent to you, you will be in bondage in your own life until you choose to forgive that person. You are not called to reconcile with the unrepentant one. You forgive others for God's sake and for your own sake. The unrepentant person will have destructive power over you in your life if you do not choose to forgive him or her for yourself. God wants us to forgive for His sake to keep in mind that there is always a bigger battle out there—one between God and Satan. Not to forgive is to give Satan glory rather than God. Unforgiveness exalts the power of evil and minimizes the power of love. God calls us to forgive people for their sake if they show us their repentance.

While God forgives immediately and completely, forgiveness is an ongoing process for us as mere humans. Forgiveness does not produce immediate change, but is a progression of identifying the injury, identifying feelings resulting from the injury, sharing feelings with safe people, setting boundaries, and finally canceling the debt. Forgiveness ultimately desires reconciliation.

Perseverance

The journey of healing is one that demands perseverance.

> Not only so, but we also rejoice in our sufferings, because we know that suffering produces perseverance; perseverance, character; and character, hope. (Romans 5:3-4)

God tests us through the healing process in order to build character.

> God "will give to each person according to what he has done." To those who by persistence in doing good seek glory, honor and immortality, he will give eternal life. But for those who are self-seeking and who reject the truth and follow evil, there will be wrath and anger. (Romans 2:6-8)

Again the themes of this book are being reiterated. God longs for us to follow His way, and when we choose a path of our own way—a self-seeking path—we will lose God's grace and kindness. Again Paul talks about our need to persevere:

> We ought always to thank God for you, brothers, and rightly so, because your faith is growing more and more, and the love every one of you has for each other is increasing.

> Therefore, among God's churches we boast about your perseverance and faith in all the persecutions and trials you are enduring. All this is evidence that God's judgment is right, and as a result you will be counted worthy of the kingdom of God, for which you are suffering. God is just. He will pay back trouble to those who trouble you and give relief to you who are troubled, and to us as well. (2 Thessalonians 1:3-7)

This passage emphasizes that our perseverance may pay off only in heaven when God's righteousness will be revealed. May we all choose to be called heroes of the faith, whether we receive fulfillment on this earth or not.

Finally, our success in persisting in the change process depends wholly upon our willingness to maintain focus on Jesus Christ. "Let us fix our eyes on Jesus, the author and perfector of our faith..." (Hebrews 12:2-3). Without Christ our healing is ever incomplete, but through Christ we may experience the rich, deep blessings of emotional healing God's way.

Co-depence:
try living overly dependant on someone else
trying to control others for own benefit.